Your View of God... God's View of You

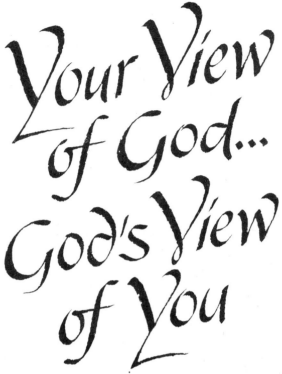

Your View of God... God's View of You

INSPIRATIONAL DEVOTIONS FOR WOMEN

by
Kathy Collard Miller

BEACON HILL PRESS OF KANSAS CITY
Kansas City, Missouri

Copyright 1992
by Beacon Hill Press of Kansas City

ISBN: 083-411-4313

Printed in the
United States of America

Cover Design: Crandall Vail

10   9   8   7   6   5   4   3   2   1

This book is lovingly dedicated
to two very special and important people in my life:
My children, Darcy and Mark.
May you see yourselves the way God sees you.

Contents

Acknowledgments

The following publishers have generously given permission to use extended quotations from copyrighted works:

From *All the Doctrines of the Bible,* by Herbert Lockyer. Copyright 1964 by Zondervan Publishing House.

From *The Bible Knowledge Commentary,* John F. Walvoord and Roy B. Zuck, eds. Copyright 1983 by Victor Books.

From *A Celebration of Praise,* by Dick Eastman. Copyright 1984 by Baker Book House.

From *Close to His Majesty,* by David C. Needham. Copyright 1987 by Multnomah Press.

From *Elemental Theology,* by Emery H. Bancroft. Copyright 1955 by Zondervan Publishing House.

From *Harper's Encyclopedia of Bible Life,* by Madeleine S. Miller and J. Lane Miller. Copyright 1978 by Harper and Row Publishers.

From *Illustrations of Bible Truth,* by H. A. Ironside. Copyright 1945 by Moody Press.

From *Knowing God,* by J. I. Packer. Copyright 1973 by Inter-Varsity Press.

From *The Knowledge of the Holy: The Attributes of God: Their Meaning in the Christian Life,* by A. W. Tozer. Copyright 1961 by Harper and Brothers, Publishers.

From *Topical Encyclopedia of Living Quotations,* Sherwood Eliot Wirt and Kersten Beckstrom, eds. Copyright 1982 by Bethany House Publishers.

From *A View from the Zoo,* by Gary Richmond. Copyright 1987 by Word Books.

Introduction

Paul wrote to the Ephesians: "I keep asking that the God of our Lord Jesus Christ, the glorious Father, may give you the Spirit of wisdom and revelation, so that you may know him better" (1:17, NIV).

James I. Packer wrote, "What makes life worth while is having a big enough objective, something which catches our imagination and lays hold of our allegiance; and this the Christian has, in a way that no other man has. For what higher, more exalted, and more compelling goal can there be than to know God?"[1]

The purpose of this book is twofold. You'll find out more about who God is and how to praise Him more knowledgeably. That is the highest calling for Christians. Yet, for many of us, that may seem like an overwhelming goal.

For a long time, when I tried to focus on who God is and praise Him, I invariably ended up thanking Him for what He had done in my life. It wasn't until I learned the difference between thanking Him and praising Him that I was able to put true praise in my devotional life.

Thanking God is concentrating on what He has done and is doing. Praising Him focuses on who He is. By doing both and not confusing the two, we can enter God's presence with greater joy because we know Him better.

You'll also discover the spiritual inheritance you have in Christ. This is God's view of you: how you are loved, accepted, and valued, and how you have received blessings like redemption, grace, forgiveness, confidence, power, and joy. Concentrating and meditating on these treasures will build your self-esteem and strengthen your ability to serve and obey God.

I encourage you to use this book during your quiet time. Choose a devotional to read as you begin your prayer time. You can either go through the devotions in order or choose a quality of God or spiritual blessing that you believe will minister to you that day. After reading the devotion, concentrate on that attribute of God and praise Him in your own words. Or if you're reading one of the spiritual blessings, thank Him for the special way He views you.

My prayer is that these devotions will open a new world of knowing God better and knowing you are "in Christ."

SECTION I

Your View
of God...

1 / God Is Love

God's love is shown by His total desire for your welfare. He is concerned about every minute detail of your life. There is nothing that you experience that is not of interest to Him. Everything God does in your life is because He wants the best for you.

"God is love. By this the love of God was manifested in us, that God has sent His only begotten Son into the world so that we might live through Him" (1 John 4:8-9, NASB).

One afternoon after I'd been a Christian for about five years, I drove home from church feeling downhearted. Why can't I love God enough? I asked myself over and over again. I was afraid that if I didn't love Him "enough," He would never fully accept me as His child.

I remembered 1 John 4:18, and it seemed to scream of my need to have a perfect love toward God: "There is no fear in love; but perfect love casts out fear."

"See, Kathy," I berated myself, "if your love for God was perfect, you wouldn't have any fear of Him."

Lord, it's just hopeless. I can never love You enough to take away this fear of what You might do to me if I don't measure up.

Then as I stopped the car at a red light, the meaning of that verse broke open in my mind like the sun bursting forth from behind a black cloud blown away by the wind. *Wait a minute, Lord. That verse isn't talking about* my *love for You, but* Your *love for me. Now I understand.* Your *perfect love can cast out* my *fear because You only want what's best for me. Oh, thank You!*

That thought revolutionized my thinking. No longer was I required to "love enough." God's unconditional and neverending love—His perfect love—could take away my fears and assure me He has only good plans in mind for me.

Charles Morgan said, "There is no surprise more wonderful than the surprise of being loved; it is God's finger on man's shoulder." That's how I felt in that moment. I was set free to receive God's unconditional love. Not a love that demands more and more—a "more" that I can't fulfill—but a love that is satisfied based on Jesus' substitutionary sacrificial death.

My friend Dawnell needed to understand that principle when she called me recently and said, "I've been reading a book that tells me to have a Christian family, but I don't know if I have one or not. How do I know?"

My heart went out to her. She was a new Christian, and I knew at the root of her question was her uneasiness about not being fully acceptable to God.

I replied, "Dawnell, you've asked a question that can't be easily answered with a list of dos and don'ts. But let me assure you, God is pleased with your desire to do the right thing. Even though you won't have a perfect Christian family, you are still completely accepted by God."

Many of us are like Dawnell. We're worried we're not performing to God's expectations and therefore won't be worthy of His love. We wonder whether we'll arrive in heaven and be stamped "Inferior product."

How wonderful it is to know that there's nothing we can do to make Him love us more, and there's nothing we can do to make Him love us less. We'll arrive in heaven, and as Jesus smiles at us, we'll feel as if He has stamped upon our foreheads, "Totally approved."

Andrew Murray said, "The love that we need is God himself coming into our hearts. When the soul is perfected in love, it has such a sense of that love it can rest in it for eternity, and though it has as much as it can contain for the time being, it can always receive more."[1]

Heavenly Father, I praise You for Your never-wavering love, which I don't need to earn. You demonstrated Your love by sending Jesus 2,000 years before I ever had an opportunity to prove my love. I'm very grateful. Because I know Your unconditional love for me, I can now love and accept others. Amen.

2 / God Is Joy

God's joy is a feeling of delight, enjoyment, or pleasure. His joy is not the fickle happiness of a human. Instead, it's never-ending because He knows in the end He'll be victorious, and everyone will recognize that He is the great King!

"The joy of the Lord is your strength" (Neh. 8:10).

"I have told you this so that my joy may be in you and that your joy may be complete" (John 15:11, NIV).

My sister-in-law, Leslie, said to me, "Kathy, you'll never guess what Chuck said about our Bible study the other night after you left our house."

I cringed inside, wondering what my brother might have said, since he didn't come to the study. "Oh, what?" I hesitantly asked, thinking maybe I shouldn't hear.

"He said, 'Boy, you guys sure laughed a lot.' Isn't that great he noticed?"

I smiled. "Leslie, you should have told him, 'Kathy was nice to us tonight; she let us get off our knees for once.'"

Leslie grinned back at me.

Chuck couldn't believe that we could have so much fun studying the Bible. Similarly, some people find it hard to believe that God is joyful.

I've been in that category before. Because of my serious nature, as a child I envisioned God as a strict taskmaster who was always frowning and saying, "You should have done better." But in the last several years, it's been easier for me to think of God as joyful and actually *smiling!*

When I watched the film *Jesus*, produced by Campus Crusade for Christ, I was impressed with how often Jesus smiled at His disciples and those around Him. I'd always pictured Jesus with a gruff facial expression as He said things like, "Now suppose one of you fathers is asked by his son for a fish; he will not give him a snake instead of a fish, will he?" (Luke 11:11).

Although the Bible doesn't tell us Jesus smiled, when I saw Jesus smiling in the film as He said those words, it seemed absolutely appropriate and changed my impression of how He might have taught. I could even believe that Jesus had a twinkle in His eye because He said something that is actually humorous: He contrasted a snake with a fish. The possibility of Jesus having a sense of humor was a new thought for me.

But how can God be so joyful when He sees people on earth rejecting Him? Because He knows the final result—that every person who ever lived will acknowledge Him as the only God. And even though everyone will not reside with Him in heaven, He will have a large group of believers who will praise Him for all eternity.

The next time you read a portion of Matthew, Mark, Luke, or John, try imagining Jesus smiling as He talks. You might get a whole new perspective of God's joyful nature, represented fully in Jesus Christ.

Pastor Paul Lee Tan writes:

> During the last 12 years of my pastorate we had a form of service in which the children came with their parents to the morning worship period. Just before the sermon they marched to their classrooms . . . past the pulpit.
>
> For me as their pastor, one of the high points of the service was the privilege of catching a smile from each child and giving one in return. I tried never to miss a single one, but one day apparently I failed. A little curly-headed four-year-old ran out of the procession and threw herself into the arms of her mother, sobbing as though her heart was broken.
>
> After the service I sought out the mother. She said that when she had quieted the little one and asked why she had cried, she received this pathetic answer. "I smiled at God, but he didn't smile back to me!"[1]

Do you feel as if God isn't smiling at you? Then consider the great joy He has in knowing you are His child. Change the image you have of Him to a joyful one—smiling at you.

———

Joyous Father, I rejoice in Your ability to have a glad heart. You know what the history of earth will be—You will be victorious. I praise You for Your joyful spirit. As a result, I can be joyful also, even in the midst of difficulty. Amen.

3 / God Is Humble

Jesus demonstrated God's humility in His willingness to lower himself to be a human being.

"Take My yoke upon you, and learn from Me, for I am gentle and humble in heart; and you shall find rest for your souls" (Matt. 11:29).

As I began my prayer time with praise, I went down the alphabet, naming God's wonderful attributes. For *a*—available; for *b*—beautiful; for *c*—compassionate. I continued on to the letter *h* and thought, *God, You're so . . . humble . . .*

I stopped abruptly. *Lord, how can You be humble? How can anyone as great and mighty and glorious as You be humble? And You know how great You are too. How can You stay humble?*

As I meditated on this, I realized God's greatness doesn't puff Him up with pride. I reminded myself of the true definition of humility: not putting yourself on the level of a worm, but thinking the truth about yourself. God correctly judges His attributes, yet He doesn't think too highly of himself (Rom. 12:3). He doesn't think more highly of himself than is correct.

Of course, with God—the Almighty God of this universe—that's a very big area. His qualities extend to the "nth" degree. He is "I am." Yet, God doesn't say that with pride, because He is telling the truth. Pride builds up beyond the truth; humility tells the truth.

Dr. J. F. Cowan once told the story of a small religious college that was having financial difficulties, even though their academic standards had been exceptionally high. One day, a very wealthy man came on the campus, found a white-haired man in overalls painting the wall, and asked where he could find the president. The painter pointed out a house on the campus and said he was sure the president could be seen there at noon.

At the designated time the visitor knocked at the president's door and was admitted by the same man he had talked to on the grounds, though now he was attired differently. The visitor accepted an invitation to have lunch with the painter-president, asked a number of questions about the needs of the college, and told him he would be sending a little donation. Two days later a letter arrived enclosing a check for $50,000. The humility of a man who was fitted for his position as college president, but who was not too proud to put on the clothes of a workman and do the job that needed to be done so badly, had opened his purse strings.

God's humility enables Him to reach out to each of us and allow us to view His greatness—that we might give Him the praise He deserves.

————

Great God, You are humble, rightly acknowledging Your greatness. Yet You were willing to associate with Your created people who are so inferior to You. I praise You and bless Your holy name. Amen.

4 / God Is Faithful

God's faithfulness makes Him dependable and reliable in everything He does in your life. You can trust Him to always do the right thing and fulfill His promises. He will do what He says.

"O Lord, Thou art my God; I will exalt Thee, I will give thanks to Thy name; for Thou hast worked wonders, plans formed long ago, with perfect faithfulness" (Isa. 25:1).

Anna Chertkova, aged 60, was released from a Soviet psychiatric hospital, ending a 14-year confinement for distributing Christian literature and openly talking about her faith. While there, she was subject to severe beatings and given forced injections of neuroleptic drugs.

After her release, she wrote her sister, saying, "Greetings, my beloved ones in the Lord. May His name be glorified worthily by us, both in our life and in our death!

"Praise God for the gift of His only-begotten Son, for the

fullness of salvation, for victory, love, and happiness in Christ . . . Thanks to His mercy, we are alive and have everything we need for life and for godly living . . . And so I cherish the time and the opportunity entrusted to me by the Lord himself. Glory to Him for everything!"

What an example of God's faithfulness! He promises to sustain us even in deep persecution and trials. And so He does, as we see so wondrously demonstrated in a 60-year-old Russian woman's life.

But for those of us in America who don't suffer this sort of persecution, how does God show His faithfulness?

Judy Downs Douglas tells of a time when her colicky infant, Debbie, screamed month after month.

> Would Debbie never sleep like other babies? Would I ever feel rested again? Would I ever sleep through the night? Would Steve and I ever have a few minutes just to talk, much less an evening to ourselves?
>
> Again the Lord Jesus assured me: "God, who has called you into fellowship with his Son Jesus Christ our Lord, is faithful" (1 Cor. 1:9, NIV). Jesus Christ was with me—for every weary moment. He was faithful to give me strength and endurance, serenity and encouragement. He would never leave me or forsake me. And He would give me rest—supernatural rest now, and sometime soon, perhaps, a good night's sleep.[1]

Beloved child of God, is there some area in which God hasn't yet shown His faithfulness to you? Rest assured, He will. For to be faithful is an integral part of His nature, and He can do no other.

Andrew Murray said, "Be assured that if God waits longer than you wish, it is only to make the blessing all the more precious. God waited 4,000 years, till the fullness of time, before He sent His Son."[2]

Precious Lord, I praise You for Your faithfulness. Even though it may seem as if You're not keeping Your promises as quickly as I'd like, I trust that You will respond to my cries in perfect faithfulness. Amen.

5 / God Is Good

God's goodness is how He makes the best decision in every area of your life. What He does brings benefit and wholeness.

"Good and upright is the Lord; therefore He instructs sinners in the way" (Ps. 25:8).

"O taste and see that the Lord is good; how blessed is the man who takes refuge in Him!" (Ps. 34:8).

When basketball star Pete Maravich died suddenly in 1988 at the age of 40, many were stunned, including me. "How can God be good?" I lamented. "Pete is serving the Lord, bringing many to Him. God can't be good to do such a horrible thing!"

After an autopsy was performed on Pete, the coroner determined he died of deterioration of the tissues in his heart because he was born without one of the two artery systems that supply the heart with blood. Doctors were amazed! Pete Maravich should not have lived to be 20, much less 40 and play record-breaking basketball.

Now God's goodness seemed vindicated. He had given Pete Maravich 20 more years than he should have had, plus the time to come to know Him as Lord and Savior in 1980.

I learned a lesson. God is always good, regardless of what I think.

We've all said things like, "The Lord is so good. He answered my prayer." Or, "The Lord is good. He provided a job." I've said those things, too, but inside I wondered, If He hadn't provided that job or answered that prayer, wouldn't He still be good?

God's goodness is not dependent upon our evaluation of how He works in our lives. That's hard to accept when we hear of thousands dying in a flood or a deranged man shooting 20 to death. "Is God good then?" we ask.

Yes, He is. This world is filled with evil and horror, but it is not of God's making. He works regardless, wanting everyone to know Him so that they can spend eternity with Him. There are no guarantees that everything we experience will measure up as "good" in our estimation.

Yet, God is still making right choices, offering love, supplying mercy, and being good.

Almighty God, I worship You, the Fountain of goodness. You desire the best for men; and even though what happens doesn't always appear to be the best, we can believe that it is if we are surrendered to Your will. Glory to Your name. Amen.

6 / God Is Truth

God knows everything, and His knowledge is based on reality and fact. His perspective is not marred or distorted by faulty thinking, but instead, God is the very essence of integrity.

"He is the Rock, his work is perfect: for all his ways are judgment: a God of truth and without iniquity, just and right is he" (Deut. 32:4, KJV).

You'd certainly expect to be able to depend upon the integrity and truth of the *Encyclopaedia Britannica*, right? Well . . .

The *Encyclopaedia Britannica* tells its readers that the Salem Church Dam on the Rappahannock River in Fredericksburg, Va., is 194 feet high and 8,850 feet long. It is located upstream from Fredericksburg and makes hydroelectric power and controls floods. But guess what? There isn't any such dam. Although an Army Corps of Engineers drew up plans for it in 1944, it was never built.

How could this mistake within such a respected encyclopedia have happened? "The whole reason for the encyclopedia is accuracy, but we are dealing with 44 million words, and we sometimes do make mistakes," says Larry Grinnell, a spokesman for *Encyclopaedia Britannica,* as quoted in the *LA Times.* "The error will be corrected in the next update possible" (*LA Times,* Aug. 18, 1988).

You and I are never going to be given an update to correct the facts about God's character or His Word. His qualities of truthfulness, love, compassion, and so many other wonderful characteristics have always been there, and they always will be. They never change. And the facts stated in His Word are timeless and immutable. We may not always understand them perfectly, and at times our explanation of them may have to be altered; but the facts themselves never change.

As Dick Eastman says, "Without the integrity of God, everything He says about Himself in His Word would be open to question."[1]

Talk about security in our lives! God's truth is a strong, rocklike foundation that will always hold us steady.

"Truth, simply stated, is a declaration of something that is absolutely right in accordance with all the facts."[2] And God knows all the facts!

Our world is full of those who claim to know the facts and who proclaim they are telling the truth, but only God can truly make that claim with full and uncompromising veracity.

———

Almighty God of truth, I praise You that only You embody all truth. I can depend on You to never make a mistake and to know all the facts. I find my security in You. Amen.

7 / God Is Encouraging

God wants us to succeed in His plan for our lives. He will do all He can to stimulate us to persevere through our trials.

"What then shall we say to these things? If God is for us, who is against us?" (Rom. 8:31).

Syd Leibovitch knew how to spell *discouragement* forward and backward on July 4, 1985, when he spent $1,500 on 750 watermelons to be distributed to homeowners in his Los Angeles area territory. After putting 500 of them on doorsteps along with a flier containing his picture and name, someone told the 24-year-old real estate agent that watermelons were being recalled for possible pesticide contamination.

"My first concern was that nobody would die or anything," he declared. So he went back to many of the homes to explain why he wanted the melons back. When he could only recover 50, he typed out another flier telling about the recall and dropped them off at the homes where he'd originally left the watermelons. By the end of the day, Syd wished he'd never heard of watermelon. His sweet idea had turned sour.

We've all felt like Syd Leibovitch. During those times it's hard to envision God wanting to encourage us. If we're so down on ourselves, how can anybody else be for us? But God values us so much that He never gives up on us, especially since He knows He has the power to help us out of our pit of discouragement.

There was a time in my life when discouragement and despair had completely eaten away at any hope left. In my book *Help for Hurting Moms,* I tell in detail about that period when I was 27 years old, my daughter, Darcy, was 2 years old, and my son, Mark, was a newborn. My husband, Larry, seemed emotionally divorced from me and totally insensitive. My anger toward him began to be displaced onto Darcy to the point that I physically abused her. "O God," I cried out often. "Why won't You deliver me from my anger? Please, take it away!"

But the anger remained. God has given up on me, I concluded. I'm beyond His help and forgiveness. I'm too bad for Him to answer my pleas. I was convinced He was no longer *for* me. Suicide seemed the only way out.

But God hadn't given up on me, and through a process of growth, He showed me the underlying causes of my anger and how to deal with them. I began to have hope again. Over time, I could truly believe He was on my side.

He can do the same for you, regardless of whether you think you deserve it or not.

In an Ann Landers column on July 11, 1988, a reader writes, "Our son's team is made up of seven- to nine-year-olds. 'Jimmy,' one of the members, is handicapped. He has Down's syndrome. The lad was up to bat, and for the first time, he hit the ball. Although he was tagged out at first base, he kept running. And then it happened. Every spectator at the game stood up to cheer him on. When Jimmy reached home base, all his teammates rushed over to give him a pat on the back and tell him he was terrific."

Maybe you feel as if you've been tagged out at first base, but God wants you to keep running. In His eyes, you're a grand slam hitter, and He knows His team is going to win the game.

Heavenly Father, thank You that You are for me, and You never give up on me. Your Spirit within me is telling me to go for it: to fulfill Your plan for me, even though there are times of discouragement and risk. Amen.

8 / God Is Omnipotent

There is nothing that God can't accomplish effectively and efficiently. He controls and directs the earth and universe.

"God hath spoken once; twice have I heard this; that power belongeth unto God" (Ps. 62:11, KJV).

"Great is our Lord, and of great power: his understanding is infinite" (Ps. 147:5, KJV).

Dick wanted out! He walked out of the marriage counselor's office where he'd gone with his wife, Janeen. What the counselor and God were asking him to do was impossible. He couldn't forgive Janeen for some things she'd done in the past—over a decade ago. Over those years, even though he was a committed Christian, he'd buried his feelings deep; but now they'd surfaced in anger and bitterness to the point that he'd begun drinking, something he'd never done before. In a rage fed by alcohol and prescription drugs, he'd thrown Janeen and their five children out of their house.

After Dick left the counseling office, the counselor told Janeen she might as well say good-bye to her marriage. He said no one as angry as Dick had ever been reconciled to their marriage.

When Dick left, he walked to the nearby freeway to hitch-hike back to his office. After many cars passed him, one car stopped, and he was offered a ride by a man who introduced himself as Jim. As they traveled down the freeway, they talked about the casual things, and then Jim asked Dick, "How come you're needing a ride?"

Dick shifted in his seat uncomfortably. "I walked out on my wife at the counselor's office."

Jim looked straight at Dick and said, "You need to get down on your knees and look to God."

Dick stared back at him in amazement. Before he could say anything else, they reached the place where Jim had to drop Dick off, and they said good-bye.

Dick walked for a while in the direction of his office with his thumb out, hoping for another ride. As he waited he told God, *Don't You dare send me another Christian to pick me up.*

When a car finally pulled over, he climbed in and met Sonny. After some small talk, Sonny asked Dick why he was walking.

Dick gulped and replied, "I left my wife at a counseling session."

Sonny stared at Dick and said, "You need to get down on your knees and look to God."

Dick's embittered heart melted. When Sonny dropped him off in front of his office, he was ready to seriously consider what God wanted him to do, eventually resulting in his forgiving Janeen and beginning an exciting new adventure of oneness in his marriage.

Dick believes that Jim and Sonny may have been angels sent by God. He acknowledges God's power and sovereignty in the healing of his marriage.

A. W. Tozer, in writing about God's power, says, "Since He has at His command all the power in the universe, the Lord God omnipotent can do anything as easily as anything else. All His acts are done without effort. He expends no energy that must be replenished. . . . All the power required to do all that He wills to do lies in undiminished fullness in His own infinite being."[1]

At times, God's use of His power seems mysterious to us because He doesn't always do everything we want. Merrill Unger speaks to that mystery: "By ascribing to God absolute power, it is not meant that God is free from all the restraints of reason and morality, as some have taught, but that He is able to do everything that is in harmony with his wise and holy and perfect nature."[2]

At a time in my life when Larry seemed completely insensitive to my cries for closeness, I prayed for God to do something dramatic to change Larry. I even gave Him permission to strike Larry with some horrible disease or paralysis. I figured then he would have to stay home. Yet God chose to change me first instead. God may not always respond with His power exactly the way we'd like, but that doesn't diminish His ability or His omnipotence. He is still powerful in His nature and knows best what to do with it.

———————

Powerful God, I praise You for Your wise use of Your omnipotence. I will continue to ask You to work in the hearts and lives of myself and others, but I surrender my desire to demand You work in a certain way. Thank You that I can trust Your mighty power, however You decide to use it. Amen.

9 / God Is Trustworthy

God knows best. He has proven himself trustworthy throughout generations of people who have looked to Him and depended on Him. He can be trusted.

"In Thee our fathers trusted; they trusted, and Thou didst deliver them. To Thee they cried out, and were delivered; in Thee they trusted, and were not disappointed" (Ps. 22:4-5).

Larry found Oscar by the gas pumps at the police station. When he brought him home, we figured he was just another stray kitten. His thin frame and filthy white fur made us sure we had rescued him from a miserable life and possible death. Darcy and Mark had been begging for a kitten; so when Larry saw this starving creature with one blue eye and one green eye, he figured he might as well give in and bring it home.

When I took Oscar to the vet for a checkup, I was surprised to learn our kitten was actually full grown and between two and five years old. As we fed Oscar regularly, he became a healthy, fat, and very handsome white cat.

I had heard of scaredy-cats, but Oscar proved himself to be the ultimate fearful cat. He would jump at the slightest sound; and we didn't dare get a plastic bag close to him, or he would run away and hide under the couch.

When our friends came to visit, Oscar quickly found a safe hiding place under a bed. We were all fascinated by his behavior and wondered if he had been abused as a kitten and then abandoned. Had someone put him in a plastic bag and tried to get rid of him? We conjectured all sorts of things that might have happened to make him so skittish.

It's been over five years since Oscar became a part of our family, and his fears have lessened only a little. When I get a plastic trash bag out of the kitchen cabinet, Oscar still runs into the other room.

"What's wrong, Oscar?" I sometimes ask him. "Do you really think I'd put you in this bag? I love you. I wouldn't do anything like that."

One day when an aluminum cooking pot slipped out of my hand and banged the floor, Oscar, who'd been eating nearby, jumped and ran. "Oscar!" I called. "I wasn't throwing it at you."

Recently I drove Oscar to the vet for a checkup and rabies shot. His plaintive cry made me question him. "I know you don't like going to the vet, but it's really for your own good. I'm sorry, Oscar, but we have to do it. It's the only way you'll stay healthy, and we want you to live a long time."

Yesterday I was walking through the family room. Oscar had been lying on the floor, dozing in the sunlight, which streamed through the sliding glass door. I reached out my hand to pet him, but he jumped to his feet, backing away from me. "Oscar, you silly. I was just going to pet you. Don't you trust me?"

"Don't you trust me?" suddenly echoed through my mind and heart. *God, You've said the same thing to me many times, haven't You? When I don't trust You, do You feel the same sadness I feel when Oscar runs away and seems afraid I'm going to hurt him? I can understand now if You do. Just as I intend only good for Oscar, even when I take him to the vet, You, my Heavenly Father, intend only good for me through the experiences You allow in my life. I wish I could convince Oscar I'm worthy of his trust. You must wonder when I'm going to learn that You also are completely worthy of my trust in every aspect of my life.*

———

Trustworthy Lord, thank You for Your patience with my fearful reactions to Your control on my life. Teach me more how to believe You can be trusted because Your touch is gentle and Your burden light. Amen.

10 / God Is Sovereign

God's sovereignty is His supreme rule over all creation and beyond. His plans will be fulfilled regardless of any obstacle or problems.

"The Lord of hosts has sworn saying, 'Surely, just as I have intended so it has happened, and just as I have planned so it will stand'" (Isa. 14:24).

"Blessed be the name of God for ever and ever: for wisdom and might are his: and he changeth the times and the seasons: he removeth kings, and setteth up kings: he giveth wisdom unto the wise, and knowledge to them that know understanding: he revealeth the deep and secret things: he knoweth what is in the darkness, and the light dwelleth with him" (Dan. 2:20-22, KJV).

I think we all wonder how we'll respond if someone we love faces a life-threatening situation. I discovered how I'd respond one Monday evening after Larry's dangerous-looking mole was removed the preceding week. Dr. Hanson called to tell Larry to come into the office the next day instead of waiting for his appointment two days later. Larry was at work, so I asked the doctor, "Then the tests are back and they've confirmed the mole was cancerous?"

Silence filled the phone line. Dr. Hanson obviously didn't want a hysterical wife on the phone.

Cautiously he answered, "Yes, it is."

My voice trembled as I asked a few more questions. He was hesitant to answer, I could tell, so I told him Larry would be there tomorrow.

I called the police department where Larry works as a sergeant, and, of course, he was out on the street as I expected. I left a message saying he should call home immediately. I knew he would know exactly what that meant.

Three minutes later when the phone rang, I answered it and told Larry, "Honey, the tests came back. It's melanoma."

There was a slight pause, and then Larry asked, "How do you feel?"

"I'm fine. We really knew it was anyway, didn't we? Now it's just confirmed."

"Yes, that's right."

We talked quietly for a few moments as I told him what sketchy information the doctor had given me.

After we hung up, I made several phone calls to individuals and prayer chains, asking them to pray for Larry's protection and safety.

Later, when Larry arrived home from work, we talked for several hours. The recurring theme we mentioned was believing

God knew exactly what He was doing. Even if God called Larry home to heaven, He was still a sovereign, wise God, and worthy of our praise and adoration.

In the following weeks, we've continued to echo that belief. God's peace and assurance of His control have empowered us to depend upon the fact that even when bad things happen, God has not stepped off His throne to tend to more important things. No, He's aware and still in charge over His creation.

A. W. Tozer expresses it this way: "His sovereignty requires that He be absolutely free, which means simply that He must be free to do whatever He wills to do anywhere at any time to carry out His eternal purpose in every single detail without interference."[1]

Within God's sovereignty He has determined that man will have free choice. At times, this seems to cancel out God's control. In addressing this conflict, Tozer responds: "God sovereignly decreed that man should be free to exercise moral choice, and man from the beginning has fulfilled that decree by making his choice between good and evil. When he chooses to do evil, he does not thereby countervail the sovereign will of God but fulfills it, inasmuch as the eternal decree decided not which choice the man should make but that he should be free to make it."[2]

As Larry and I have had a choice to make in whether to trust God for Larry's cancer, I can say with certainty that even as I've grieved over the possibility of losing my best friend, my belief that God's sovereignty is in control has not wavered. So far God has answered yes to our request for Larry's safety, as additional tests have revealed no further cancer. But even if the cancer returns, God is still on His throne.

————

Sovereign God, I worship Your rule over this world, my life, and my circumstances. Thank You that nothing enters my life except that which has already passed through the filter of Your control and love. Amen.

11 / God Is Reachable

God wants us to know who He is and that He can be reached. He desires to be real to us and for us to make Him the highest priority in our lives.

"Thus says the Lord, 'Let not a wise man boast of his wisdom, and let not the mighty man boast of his might, let not a rich man boast of his riches; but let him who boasts boast of this, that he understands and knows Me, that I am the Lord who exercises lovingkindness, justice, and righteousness on earth; for I delight in these things,' declares the Lord" (Jer. 9:23-24).

My sister Karen's journal for May 1, 1990, reads: "I've been thinking a lot about Kathy's book, *Sure Footing in a Shaky World*. She talked about *learning* to love and serve God for that alone and not just to make my life go smoothly. I look to God and pray for my family's safety and for their needs to be met, instead of seeking Him just to be close to Him. So from now on, my prayer is to learn to love and trust God no matter how difficult my life may become. This is real security."

When we talked later, Karen shared with me that she'd been concentrating on wanting to know who God is, rather than just seeking Him in order to deal with the trials in her life.

Last week, when we talked again, Karen stressed how she'd continued to seek after God just for the purpose of loving Him more. Then she told me, "As I slowly woke up the other morning, my mind seemed to think over and over again, 100, 100, 100. I thought that was funny, as if it were a broken record. Then it seemed to change slightly, and I thought of the number 119. I sensed God was speaking to me, and within a second the words *Psalm 119, verse 10* lit up in my mind. This kind of thing had never happened to me before, and I was amazed. Psalm 119, verse 10? I had never memorized that verse, didn't even know what it could possibly refer to. What was God trying to tell me?

"Of course I jumped out of bed and opened my Bible to Ps. 119:10. I read, 'With all my heart I have sought Thee; do not let me wander from Thy commandments.'

"Wow! I couldn't believe it. God was trying to tell me that I was doing the right thing by *seeking* to get to know Him. He wants to affirm that He's pleased with my desire to *seek* Him."

I was thrilled to hear my sister's story. To think that the Almighty God of this whole universe is knowable, reachable, and available impresses our human minds. Karen's experience confirmed within me, and I hope within you, dear reader, that God is reachable and that your seeking Him is not in vain, even if you don't always feel His presence.

Dear Father, to know You are right here with me and that You want me to seek after You is truly incredible. Thank You that You make yourself reachable even if I can't know You to the fullest extent. Help me to continue to seek You. Amen.

12 / God Is Patient

God has the ability to wait for the results of His efforts and plans. With great self-control, He steadily continues His work without intolerance or anger.

"But thou, O Lord, art a God full of compassion, and gracious, longsuffering, and plenteous in mercy and truth" (Ps. 86:15, KJV).

"For I am confident of this very thing, that He who began a good work in you will perfect it until the day of Christ Jesus" (Phil. 1:6).

Sometimes I think if God weren't so patient, things would get done faster. But then I remember what Dr. A. H. Strong said: "When God wants to make an oak, He takes a hundred years; but when He wants to make a squash, He takes six months." So I must admit that maybe He knows what He's doing.

I can certainly see the results of His patience as I flip through the Bible. Here are some examples of God's patient dealings with men:

God took six days to create our world, when He could have called it into existence in one second.

God provided Noah 120 years to build the ark and give people an opportunity to turn to Him.

God caused Isaac to be born to Abraham 25 years after He promised it would happen.

God took almost two decades for Joseph to see his dreams of greatness come true.

Moses spent 40 years in the wilderness being groomed to be a great leader.

God patiently disciplined the Israelites for 40 years in the wilderness.

Joshua spent many years as Moses' number one man before he was called to be head of the Israelites.

David wandered in the wilderness for over a decade before his rightful place as king was fulfilled.

The Old Testament prophets never saw most of their prophecies fulfilled in their lifetimes.

God waited 400 years between the last Old Testament prophets and the coming of Jesus.

Jesus didn't start His ministry until the age of 30.

It took 14 years after the apostle Paul was converted before God used him extensively in missionary work.

At times, it's hard for us to understand God's patience because we humans concentrate so much on instantaneous results. The concept that God doesn't move within the confines of time can help us comprehend His long-suffering nature.

> Because God lives in an everlasting now, He has no past and no future. When time-words occur in the Scriptures they refer to our time, not to His. . . .

> God dwells in eternity but time dwells in God. He has already lived all our tomorrows as He has lived all our yesterdays. . . .

> . . . Changes take place not all at once but in succession, one after the other, and it is the relation of "after" to

"before" that gives us our idea of time. We wait for the sun to move from east to west or for the hour hand to move around the face of the clock, but God is not compelled so to wait. For Him everything that will happen has already happened.[1]

God is patient because He already knows what's going to happen. You and I are impatient because we don't know but we want to. And while events unfold and people change, it seems as if it's taking forever.

God is patient because He sees the value in man's journey through circumstances that result in growth. Because God never changes, He doesn't need time. Only we finite creatures require time to measure our lives and to move through a process of growth.

God sees the end from the beginning. He knows He'll victoriously fulfill His promises and the plans He intends. No need to hurry or worry for Him!

How good for us to learn the wisdom contained in Ps. 90:12: "So teach us to number our days, that we may apply our hearts unto wisdom" (KJV).

————————

Father, how patient You are with me. I'm so grateful. Otherwise You would have given up on me long ago. I appreciate Your faithful workings in my life, even when it seems (at least to me) to take so long. Amen.

13 / God Is Creative

God's creativity enables Him to create something out of nothing, to maneuver painful life circumstances into benefit, and to cause His will to be done, even in seemingly impossible situations.

"Surely My hand founded the earth, and My right hand spread out the heavens; when I call to them, they stand together" (Isa. 48:13).

A friend recently painted a small canvas for me, showing a sailboat leaving a harbor and sailing out to sea. The painting sat propped in my living room, and as I viewed it from a distance, it was beautiful. But when I moved up close to admire it, I suddenly noticed a brushstroke of green that didn't quite fit. There were also other colors that didn't seem to blend well. Why, I didn't notice those before, I thought. But when I moved back from the picture, the "flaws" disappeared. *What seem to be mistakes blend together to make a lovely picture.*

Later that day, I looked through my journal from several years before and read of the fears, worries, and traumas that were happening at that time. I was waiting to hear from a publisher about a book proposal. My son, Mark, was suffering from continual ear infections, and we were considering having tubes put in his ears. Darcy's teacher was hinting that it might be a good idea for her to be kept back a grade in school.

The passage of time has now allowed me to stand back from those circumstances and see God's creative touch. Those situations have blended into a beautiful picture of growth and trust in the Lord. I didn't know what God was going to do at the time, but now I can see how He worked through them all. The book was accepted, not by that publisher, but by another one. My son's ears healed without surgery. Darcy moved ahead in school and is doing very well.

Slowly, I began to understand how circumstances are God's tools of creativity as He lovingly wields the brush upon the canvas of my life. In difficult times, I only see the yellow glob of grief, the blue streak of illness, and the green smudge of confusion. I view the picture up close and cry out, *O God, not that color there. Why, Lord, did that happen? That can't possibly work out for good. Can't You find a different way to move in that situation?*

Now, as God continues painting my life, I can stand back and see how I have matured and been strengthened in my faith because of His creative touch. As a result, Jer. 29:11 has become very special to me: "'For I know the plans that I have for you,' declares the Lord, 'plans for welfare and not for calamity to give you a future and a hope.'"

The next time God's creativity seems to go haywire, be assured He knows what He's doing on the canvas of your life. The picture will turn into something beautiful as you cooperate with Him. The different colors will blend together to create sense and beauty.

———————

Creative God, I stand amazed at the infinite ways You express Your ingenuity. I want Your touch of ingenuity in my life. I hand over my life's canvas and ask You to paint however You will. Help me to stay on Your easel. Amen.

14 / God Is Majestic

Recognizing God's majesty is acknowledging His greatness and His qualities of royalty, dignity, and sovereign grandeur.

"Thine, O Lord, is the greatness and the power and the glory and the victory and the majesty, indeed everything that is in the heavens and the earth; Thine is the dominion, O Lord, and Thou dost exalt Thyself as head over all. . . . and Thou dost rule over all" (1 Chron. 29:11-12).

Like me, do you sometimes have trouble comprehending the majesty of God? Our minds can't grasp God's greatness and supremacy. I even have a hard time understanding the "new math" my children bring home from school, and I loved math when I was in school! How much greater is my confusion in trying to absorb God's wonder, vastness, and immensity. He's incredible!

Regardless of my lack of understanding of God's magnificence, He does indeed want me to concentrate on His majestic nature and His fabulous touch upon my life, in my world, and in the universe.

J. I. Packer writes:

> The Christian's instincts of trust and worship are stimulated very powerfully by knowledge of the greatness of God.
>
> But this is knowledge which Christians today largely lack: and that is one reason why our faith is so feeble and our worship so flabby. We are modern men, and modern men, though they cherish great thoughts of man, as a rule have small thoughts of God. . . .
>
> Today, vast stress is laid on the thought that God is *personal*, but this truth is so stated as to leave the impression that God is a person of the same sort as we are—weak, inadequate, ineffective, a little pathetic. But this is not the God of the Bible! . . . Like us He is personal, but unlike us He is *great*.[1]

How can we keep our minds riveted on God's majesty while continuing to enjoy His person? Packer makes two suggestions: The first is to *remove from our thoughts of God the limits that would make Him small*. The second is to *compare Him with powers and forces which we regard as great*.[2]

To accomplish the first, we need to reject any thought of God that puts Him at our level. Yes, He is personally involved and interested in our world and in our individual lives, but that doesn't mean He has left His throne in heaven. We must rebuke thoughts that suggest He gets tired like us. We must throw out ideas that He can't handle all the problems from all over the earth (I won't pray about this problem. It's too small for God to pay attention to). We must discard any impression that God isn't aware of every action, thought, and decision every person of the earth makes (I'll just go ahead and make this one bad choice; God won't notice).

These subtle images limit our great God. Isaiah says, "Do you not know? Have you not heard? The Everlasting God, the Lord, the Creator of the ends of the earth does not become weary or tired. His understanding is inscrutable" (40:28).

To make Packer's second suggestion a reality in our lives,

we can consider the majestic creation of God and realize His handiwork doesn't even begin to credit Him with all the greatness He contains.

Just contemplate the wonder of your heart. It beats an average of 70 times a minute, nearly 40 million times a year, or over 2½ billion times in 70 years. As it beats, it discharges nearly 2,000 gallons a day or 650,000 gallons a year—enough to fill more than 81 tank cars of 8,000 gallons each.

As if that's not enough, meditate on the miracle of the eye. In the dark, its sensitivity increases 100,000 times. Our eye can detect a faint glow less than a thousandth as bright as a candle's flame or see light from the stars 25 billion miles away.

Then there's the ear. The inner ear is like a keyboard with 15,000 keys detecting as many different tones.

Added to that is the brain. Even though it will forget more than 90 percent of what you learn during your lifetime, it will store as much as 10 times more information than is contained in the Library of Congress with its 17 million volumes.

In chapters 38 through 41 of Job, God points out to Job and his "friends" His majestic control over the universe, saying, "Where were you when I laid the foundation of the earth! . . . Who set its measurements, since you know? Or who stretched the line on it? On what were its bases sunk? Or who laid its cornerstone, when the morning stars sang together, and all the sons of God shouted for joy?" (38:4-7).

He continues by referring to the sea, clouds, darkness, the morning and dawn, the dwelling of light and darkness, the storehouses of snow and hail, thunderbolts, frost, stars, constellations, lions, ravens, donkeys, ostriches' wings, and a plethora of others. On and on He continues until Job, overwhelmed, answers, "Behold, I am insignificant; what can I reply to Thee? I lay my hand on my mouth" (40:4).

After God points out more of His majesty, Job's final comment is, "I know that Thou canst do all things, and that no purpose of Thine can be thwarted" (42:2).

God doesn't directly answer Job's questions, instead He tells of His fantastic majestic creative powers. God proves He is far above what man can imagine of Him.

Yet, because of Almighty God's personalness, He does

reach out to Job, giving him an audience with himself. That satisfies Job, even though his questions remain unanswered.

For us, as we face troubles, it's often enough just to know God hasn't forgotten about us, even when He doesn't answer the "whys" of life.

————————

Majestic Sovereign, I bow before You, acknowledging Your royalty and dominion. I do not deserve to come before Your throne; regardless, You bid me come to worship and adore You. Thank You. Amen.

15 / God Is Mighty

God's might is His strength, authority, and power.

"The Lord thy God in the midst of thee is mighty; he will save, he will rejoice over thee with joy; he will rest in his love, he will joy over thee with singing" (Zeph. 3:17, KJV).

Lille Diane was a member of a dysfunctional family. Her stepfather sexually and emotionally abused her. She felt completely alone and abandoned. One of the few positive recollections of her childhood is when a schoolteacher heard her sing and said, "Wow, you really can sing!" That bolstered her hungry heart for a short time.

But when her mother refused to heed Lille's plea to protect her from her stepfather's molestation, teenage Lille ran away from home. She turned to drugs and alcohol and was finally placed in the California Youth Authority.

One evening as she sat staring out the window, she prayed, *God, help me.* He seemed to be her only hope, since a judge was close to placing her permanently in a CYA detention center.

Lille didn't know it, but even as she prayed, a foster mother prayed for God to direct them to whoever He would want them to bring into their home. The next day the social worker convinced the judge to give Lille one last chance. The judge assigned her to that Christian foster mother's home. After showing Lille unconditional love, that foster mother led her in prayer to become a Christian.

Lille grew strong in her faith. But after graduating from high school with honors and being out on her own, she rejected what she'd learned and returned to a destructive life-style.

She married an alcoholic and had a son, but her marriage crumbled. Her husband proved her an unfit mother during their divorce, and he received custody of their son. She was alone again.

After meeting and marrying Tom Greder, she sang professionally in a band—usually in bars. She began to recognize the addictions in their lives: cocaine, alcohol, and cigarettes. Then she was offered a $50.00 course that guaranteed she'd be freed of those compulsions. She and Tom attended their first Dianetics course and were delivered from their outward problems. They hungered for more and were drawn more and more into Scientology until they were bankrupt from paying for each successive course that promised perfection.

Her foster mother continued to pray for her, and eventually Lille's eyes were opened. She convinced Tom to leave the control of the Scientology group, even though the officials threatened their lives.

Later she became the owner of a flower shop. She unknowingly hired a group of Christians; and as they began to share God's love with her, she turned back to Jehovah's care. It was then she realized that her foster mother had continued to pray for her all those years, eventually seeing the fruit of her prayers and God's mighty hand to restore.

Today, Lille Diane and Tom Greder live in Oak View, Calif., with their four-year-old son. As a professional Christian singer, Lille shares her dynamic story and beautiful songs with many.

Lille says, "I'm a living testimony of God's mighty working power. Only He could have saved me and then drawn me back to himself after all I've been through. There's always hope with Him because He is strong and great."

16 / God Is Omnipresent

Though we humans cannot be everywhere at once, God can. He is not limited by space and has no constraints or boundaries. Because He is a Spirit, He encompasses the entire universe and beyond.

"'Am I a God who is near,' declares the Lord, 'and not a God far off? Can a man hide himself in hiding places, so I do not see him?' declares the Lord. 'Do I not fill the heavens and the earth?' declares the Lord" (Jer. 23:23-24).

In his book *Close to His Majesty,* David C. Needham tells this story:

Our home is on a hillside a few blocks from an elementary school. When our son, Greg, was attending the school, my wife, Mary Jo, occasionally would look down to the school playground to see if she could spot our little boy. It was not too difficult to pick him out among all those little bodies scurrying about. Sometimes when she looked, she would suddenly see, among hundreds of children, one little hand raised high, waving toward the house. Because of the glare on the windows, it was impossible for Greg to see her from the playground, but he simply assumed his mom was there and would be waving back.[1]

Although that mother could not be at the window constantly, God is watching us constantly, ever-present with you and me.

At times, though, we're not convinced He's close by because the window of painful circumstances is only reflecting back to us our own hurt, thus blocking our view of Him.

At those times it may seem to us that God is distant and disinterested in our lives. After all, if He is really with me, why am I going through such a trial? And if He sees my struggle, why doesn't He immediately deliver me? Our conclusion can quickly become, I must not deserve His attention, or, I'm not important enough for Him to notice my pain. Continuing in this line of reasoning, we perceive God as being aloof.

God can also appear remote to us if a prayer isn't answered immediately or the reply is "no" or "wait." And when our temptation or trial continues indefinitely, it could seem God is far away.

Fortunately, our feelings have nothing to do with God's omnipresence. It takes faith during those hard times to trust that God is near and alert to our struggle.

The truths in Scripture can help strengthen that faith, which will enable us to sense His presence. David wrote, "Where can I go from your Spirit? Where can I flee from your presence? If I go up to the heavens, you are there; if I make my bed in the depths, you are there. If I rise on the wings of the dawn, if I settle on the far side of the sea, even there your hand will guide me, your right hand will hold me fast" (Ps. 139:7-10, NIV).

His presence is based on His very being—who He is. "For the Lord will not abandon His people on account of His great name" (1 Sam. 12:22).

In times of doubt, when we ask along with the heathen philosopher, "Where is God?" we can reply with the man of faith, "Where is He not?"

Then our voices can join with Thomas Chalmers in saying:

> When I walk by the wayside, He is along with me; when I enter into company amid all my forgetfulness of Him, He never forgets me; in the silent watches of the night, when my eyelids have closed, and my spirit has sunk into unconsciousness, the observant eye of Him, who never slumbers, is upon me; I cannot flee from His presence, go where I will; He leads me, and watches me, and cares for me; and the same Being who is now at work

in the remotest domains of nature and of Providence, is also at my hand, to eke out to me every moment of my being, and to uphold me in the exercise of all my feelings, and of all my facilities."[2]

Omnipresent God, I praise You for Your incredible ability to be everywhere at once. Though my mind can't comprehend it and I don't always feel the reality of it, I choose to believe that You are with me at all times. Amen.

17 / God Is Omniscient

God knows everything. There isn't anything—past, present, or future—He doesn't know.

"Oh, the depth of the riches both of the wisdom and knowledge of God!" (Rom. 11:33).

On Sunday, the last day of the women's retreat where I was a speaker, I sat at the book table, selling and autographing books. Kris came up and bought a copy of *Sure Footing in a Shaky World*, and I began autographing it for her.

"Oh, no, wait!" she exclaimed. "I'm not buying it for myself but for a friend. I want it autographed to her."

I'd only written down "Kris," so I said, "Oh, I'm sorry, I'll get another one for you." I put the book aside and autographed another for her friend. A while later, I packed the book with the "mistake" into my briefcase and drove away, the briefcase beside me in the front seat.

A few minutes later, I thought about how good a diet soda would taste, but I didn't think I'd stop. Better to head straight home. No, I'd sure like something to drink. I will stop. There were two different routes I could take, but remembering a drive-through hamburger place I'd seen on the way, I decided to drive that way.

Pulling up to the drive-in window, I ordered a diet Pepsi and gave the young woman my money. She smiled and said, "I see you're dressed up. Did you just come from church?"

"No," I replied, "I'm coming home from speaking at a women's retreat. Do you go to church?"

"Usually I do, but I couldn't today because I had to work."

We started talking, and I inquired about her faith in God. She said she was a Christian, and we talked briefly. In a few minutes, she turned away to get my drink, and I heard God whisper in my heart, "Give her the book."

I looked at my briefcase and wondered how I'd explain to her that someone else's name was in it. I'll tell her that's how I can give it to her free—because of the autographing mistake. *OK, Lord, I'll be glad to do that.*

I retrieved the book. Wouldn't it be a coincidence if her name was Kris? Oh, sure, Kathy, dream on! I smiled at the far-fetched idea.

The woman came back to the window and handed me the cup. I spoke up. "Remember how I told you I was the speaker at that retreat? Well, I'm also an author, and I'd like to give you a copy of my book. By the way, what's your name?"

She smiled at the prospect of getting a book and answered, "My name's Kris."

I laughed and explained the situation. "I guess God wants you to have this."

A few minutes later I drove away, marveling at God's handiwork. *Incredible! God, You do know everything! You knew from the foundation of the earth that You wanted Kris to have that book, and You made it possible in a unique way. I hope she feels very special because You've shown Your love in a wondrous way.*

Even though we believe God knows everything, why is it we still think we can hide things from Him?

David Needham writes:

> Think of it! We have a God with whom we can be totally honest—utterly transparent—not only because He knows everything already, but also because He truly understands. No need to put on a false front before Him—

trying to say the right words when we pray. Appearing pious when we are actually struggling with doubts. No matter how we feel we can tell Him. Even if we are right in the middle of sinning, He is still there. He is fully understanding (grieving, but not condemning), eager to forgive and to heal.[1]

Not only does God know and understand because of His omniscience, He knows and understands because Jesus has experienced being human.

David Needham goes on to say, "Jesus, my great High Priest, has actually felt every pressure, every temptation, every weakness I will ever know. What a huge price He paid even before He went to the cross. How strange it must have been for Him to suffer through all those years of human frailty. And why? So that when you and I approach His throne we will never tell Him something that will be foreign to Him."[2]

So there's good news and bad news. The bad news is: God knows every nook and cranny of our lives. And the good news is: God knows every nook and cranny of our lives . . . and still loves us.

Just ask Kris at the hamburger place.

———————

All-knowing God, I'm amazed at Your knowledge and grateful for Your understanding. Help me to be open and vulnerable with You, for You know already what I might try to hide. Amen.

18 / God Is Eternal

God was not made or created, nor did He have a beginning. He has existed and will exist for all eternity. God, who created time, is completely untethered by it.

"Of old Thou didst found the earth; and the heavens are the work of Thy hands. Even they will perish, but Thou dost endure; and all of them will wear out like a garment; like clothing Thou wilt change them, and they will be changed. But Thou art the same, and Thy years will not come to an end" (Ps. 102:25-27).

"Even from everlasting to everlasting, Thou art God" (Ps. 90:2).

Most parents dread the day their child will ask one of two questions: "How can God live forever?" or "How long is eternity?"

How can we answer such questions when our own adult minds cannot fathom such incredible concepts?

It helps us little to say God was from the beginning. "When was the beginning?" they ask. "And by the way, how long is forever?"

Eternity can be defined as infinite duration. But don't tell your kids that. Their next question will be, "What does infinite mean?"

David Needham gives us some insight when he writes:

> With God, there is no succession of moments. There is neither future nor past. He sees everything as one eternal *now*. He can see the whole play of history—all of it— in action right now. He doesn't have to look back. He doesn't need to look ahead. He just sees it, with the end as much immediate to Him as the beginning.
>
> That's so hard to grasp! You and I aren't wired to handle a concept like this. Our mental circuit breakers trip the moment we try to wrap our minds around it. That is because we were built to operate within a *particular succession of moments*. Anything outside of this frame of reference makes us uncomfortable.[1]

That's certainly true. When we can't comprehend the eternity of God, we try to avoid the topic completely. Yet, when we consider this characteristic of God, it can actually bring us comfort. Moses' words tell us, "There is none like the God of Jeshurun, who rides the heavens to your help, and through the skies in His majesty. The eternal God is a dwelling place, and underneath are the everlasting arms; and He drove out the enemy from before you, and said, 'Destroy!' So Israel dwells in security" (Deut. 33:26-28).

We may not be able to fully comprehend God's eternal being, but the reality of His eternity can bring us strength and security. God is always there. He is not a fickle God who comes and goes, leaving us wondering if He'll be there for us. Even when we die, that next second we will be in His presence.

His eternal quality transcends time but does not prevent Him from being present with us this very moment. Isa. 57:15 tells us, "For thus says the high and exalted One who lives forever, whose name is Holy, 'I dwell on a high and holy place, and also with the contrite and lowly of spirit in order to revive the spirit of the lowly and to revive the heart of the contrite.'"

God is not contained by time, yet He goes through time with us. He knows everything that has ever happened, what is happening now, and all that will ever happen.

The next time your child asks you about eternity, just say, "It's the same as googolplexes." Oh, you don't know about that? "Googol" is the number one, followed by 100 zeros. Pretty large, huh? But the googolplex is even larger. That's "a googol raised to the googolth power." Such a number cannot be written out, for earth cannot contain the pages required for it.

And after googolplexes of years are used up—God will still be there!

————

Eternal God, my mind cannot comprehend Your never-ending existence. But I find great security in knowing You're always there and know my future. Amen.

19 / God Is Forgiving

God not only pardons us of our wrongdoings but also forgets the offense once it's pardoned.

"For Thou, Lord, art good, and ready to forgive, and abundant in lovingkindness to all who call upon Thee" (Ps. 86:5).

When anger ruled my life and I was an abusive mother, I was overwhelmed by the belief that God didn't want to forgive me. How can God offer me forgiveness? I wondered. Doesn't He say in Matt. 18:6 that anyone who misleads a child should have a bag of boulders tied around his neck and be thrown into the sea? My sin is beyond forgiveness, even God's forgiveness.

For many months, I felt hopeless and helpless, even suicidal. Yet, God demonstrated His faithfulness by pulling me from my pit of destruction and setting me upon the rock of Jesus Christ. During that time, He convinced me He desired to forgive me.

While looking through my Bible one day, Isa. 43:25 jumped out at me: "I, even I, am the one who wipes out your transgressions for My own sake; and I will not remember your sins."

"Wipes out your transgressions for My own sake"? For His own sake? My mind could not comprehend that new thought. *You mean, Lord, that You want to forgive me not just for my sake but for Your sake as well?* Something clicked within me. *I've always felt so selfish asking for Your forgiveness because it's so beneficial to me. Yet You're saying You want to forgive me because it's beneficial to You also.*

How is it beneficial to You, Lord? I thought of how forgiveness restores my relationship with Him. *That must be it! You want my fellowship. You want my company, my praise and adoration, and I can't give it to You unless I'm cleansed from sin. Ah, that's it!*

This discussion with the Lord somehow set my heart free to believe He indeed wanted to forgive me. Isa. 30:18 confirmed this: "Therefore the Lord longs to be gracious to you, and therefore He waits on high to have compassion on you. For the Lord is a God of justice; how blessed are all those who long for Him."

I knew I wanted to be among those who longed for Him, and one of the ways I could do that was by accepting His compassion wrapped in His gift of forgiveness. From that point, I was able to believe God wanted to forgive me.

A. W. Tozer explains how that was possible even though my sin was so grievous.

> But sin has made us timid and self-conscious, as well it might. Years of rebellion against God have bred in us a fear that cannot be overcome in a day. The captured rebel does not enter willingly the presence of the king he has so long fought unsuccessfully to overthrow. But if he is truly

penitent he may come, trusting only in the loving-kindness of his Lord, and the past will not be held against him. Meister Eckhart encourages us to remember that, when we return to God, even if our sins were as great in number as all mankind's put together, still God would not count them against us, but would have as much confidence in us as if we had never sinned.[1]

God's forgiveness, however, is more than just an outworking of His desire. It's based on Christ's substitutionary death on the Cross. Without Jesus' death, God could not forgive me or you.

As Oswald Chambers says, "Never build your preaching of forgiveness on the fact that God is our Father and He will forgive us because He loves . . . It is shallow nonsense to say that God forgives us because He is love. The only ground on which God can forgive me is through the cross of my Lord."[2]

H. A. Ironside told a story that illustrates how Jesus made it possible for God to put His forgiveness into action. He tells of pioneers traveling across the central states, headed for homesteading land. One day they were horrified to see a long line of smoke in the west, and they knew a prairie fire was burning out of control ahead of them. Pushed toward them by the wind, it would soon be upon them.

One man seemed to know how to save them. Telling the people to set fire to the grass behind them, a space was opened up, and they moved into its smoking blackness.

The fire from the west roared close but died out as it reached the already-burned area. The wise man told the relieved pioneers, "See? The flames cannot reach us here, for we are standing where the fire has been."[3]

Jesus cleared the way to make forgiveness possible by dying on the Cross in our place. All we need do is step into the position of accepting Him as our Substitute and believe the fire of God's wrath toward unbelievers can no longer reach us. As we stand in that smoldering, already-burned place, the smoke around us wafts upward, representing our thanksgiving and praise to God.

———

Forgiving God, thank You that You long to forgive me and set me right with You. I praise You for devising a way for Jesus to burn away the sin in my heart so that judgment cannot reach me. Amen.

20 / God Is Holy

God's primary attribute is His holiness. He is completely free from any evil and, as a result, He abhors sin.

"I saw the Lord sitting on a throne, lofty and exalted, with the train of His robe filling the temple. Seraphim stood above Him, each having six wings; with two he covered his face, and with two he covered his feet, and with two he flew. And one called out to another and said, 'Holy, Holy, Holy, is the Lord of hosts, the whole earth is full of His glory'" (Isa. 6:1-3).

Sitting here in my brightly lit bedroom, working at my computer, it's difficult for me to identify with Isaiah's awesome experience of seeing God and hearing the seraphim extol His holiness. Yet, to a small degree, I can relate with Isaiah in his response of "Woe is me, for I am ruined! Because I am a man of unclean lips, and I live among a people of unclean lips; for my eyes have seen the King, the Lord of hosts" (v. 5).

As I think of the holiness of God, I am awestruck. I cannot comprehend the full meaning of God's holiness. Imagine, to be completely without any sin. To never act in an improper way. To never have wrong motives or impure thought. Perfection is holiness, and God is perfectly holy.

Dr. Herbert Lockyer comments:

He is holy in His nature. As light is the essence of the sun, so holiness is God's very being. Because of His divine perfection, "God is absolutely distinct from all His creatures, and above them in infinite majesty" (Exod. 15:11; Isa. 57:15). He is holy in all His ways. He cannot act contrary to His nature. As the sun cannot darken, so God cannot act unrighteously. "He is the Holy One" (Job 6:10). Holiness is His inward character—not merely a trait of His Being, but His very essence—not one of a list of virtues but the sum of all excellencies rather than an excellence.[1]

Isa. 57:15 (NKJV) tells us, "For thus says the High and Lofty One who inhabits eternity, whose name is Holy: 'I dwell in the high and holy place.'"

I once heard of a Bible college professor who required his students to spend a minimum of 15 minutes lying on their backs, looking up at the stars and contemplating the holiness of God. What a wonderful idea.

In his book *The Knowledge of the Holy*, A. W. Tozer writes, "Holy is the way God is. To be holy He does not conform to a standard. He is that standard. He is absolutely holy with an infinite, incomprehensible fullness of purity that is incapable of being other than it is."[2]

He explains how we Christians should respond to the divine Holy One:

> We must like Moses cover ourselves with faith and humility while we steal a quick look at the God whom no man can see and live. The broken and the contrite heart He will not despise. We must hide our unholiness in the wounds of Christ as Moses hid himself in the cleft of the rock while the glory of God passed by. We must take refuge from God in God. Above all we must believe that God sees us perfect in His Son while He disciplines and chastens and purges us that we may be partakers of His holiness.[3]

I must confess that in my comfortableness with God as my Friend, I do not regard His holiness seriously enough. If I could comprehend His holiness, I would be compelled to hate sin as much as He does.

It appears from the state of our American society, even within the body of Christian believers, that this is a common problem. We do not fall to our faces, prostrate on the floor, when meditating on God's awesome purity. At times we preach so endlessly about His love that the absence of sin in His being is hardly mentioned.

When witnessing to unbelievers, I've sometimes fallen into the trap of speaking of His love and goodness, but being afraid to mention His holiness, thinking I might scare them away. In retrospect, maybe such knowledge would create a reverence that would bring them to true worship.

My desire is to sing that same song and to be so awestruck by God's holiness that I join the Jews who considered God's name Yahweh so sacred that they refused to pronounce it.

Instead, one day when I stand before God's throne as Isaiah did, my voice will sing out joining the seraphim, "Holy, Holy, Holy." In that moment, no other descriptive word will seem adequate.

Holy God, I bow before You in humble acknowledgment of Your purity. Help me to comprehend the awesome glory of Your holiness. Cause me to not take lightly Your sinlessness. Amen.

21 / God Is Merciful

Mercy is God relieving the misery caused by sin. It's His goodness in action toward those hurting.

"Then David said to Gad, 'I am in great distress. Let us now fall into the hand of the Lord for His mercies are great, but do not let me fall into the hand of man'" (2 Sam. 24:14).

I've been told that the river leaving Niagara Falls has some interesting safeguards for any who might fall into the river and be swept away. At several places down the river, walkways extend across the river with ropes hanging down into the water. Each knotted rope gives any poor soul being tossed down the river an opportunity to grab hold and stop his descent to destruction.

These opportunities to be saved from the rushing river are a fitting example of God's mercy. Dick Eastman defines mercy as "God being full of, or containing all the possible second chances any of us could ever need. Because all of His attributes are inexhaustible, His supply of second chances is inexhaustible."[1]

Then Dick shares with us John Bisagno's definition of the difference between love and mercy: "Love, then, is that feeling God has toward us, whom He has created. Mercy, on the other hand, is an attitude He takes toward us who are not worthy of His pardon."[2]

Deut. 4:29-31 tells us about this kind of love and mercy. "But if from there you seek the Lord your God, you will find him if you look for him with all your heart and with all your soul. When you are in distress and all these things have happened to you, then in later days you will return to the Lord your God and obey him. For the Lord your God is a merciful God; he will not abandon or destroy you or forget the covenant with your forefathers, which he confirmed to them by oath" (NIV).

Have you seen God's mercy in your life lately? God exhibits His mercy more often than we realize.

There are so many times I deserve judgment, yet God in His mercy holds out a rope of compassion and forgiveness so that I might not be destroyed.

J. A. Clarks shares this story:

When God was about to create man, says a Jewish legend, He took into His counsel the angels that stood about his throne. "Create him not," said the angel of Justice, "for if Thou dost he will commit all kinds of wickedness against his fellow men; he will be hard and cruel and dishonest and unrighteous."

"Create him not," said the angel of Truth, "for he will be false and deceitful to his brother-man, and even to Thee."

"Create him not," said the angel of Holiness; "he will follow that which is impure in Thy sight, and dishonor Thee to thy face."

Then stepped forward the angel of Mercy (God's best beloved) and said, "Create him, our Heavenly Father, for when he sins and turns from the path of right and truth and holiness I will take him tenderly by the hand, and speak loving words to him, and then lead him back to Thee."[3]

Merciful God, I so appreciate Your gift of many chances. You never give up on me and always want to restore fellowship with me. In my misery and dismay, You reach out with Your mercy. Amen.

22 / God Is Just

Justice is fairness. In God's justice, He does everything fairly and equitably. He cannot act other than with integrity.

"He will do no injustice. Every morning He brings His justice to light; He does not fail. But the unjust knows no shame" (Zeph. 3:5).

Do you know how a giraffe is born? I would have thought the mother giraffe would lie down, and the baby would slide out onto solid ground. But that's not the way it is. God designed a giraffe's birth in what would seem a totally cruel way: the mother giraffe stands up as the calf is born, thus causing the baby to fall 10 feet to the ground. Gary Richmond, in his book *A View from the Zoo*, gives an accounting of the birth of a giraffe.

> The moment we had anticipated was not a disappointment. The calf, a plucky male, hurled forth, falling 10 feet and landing on his back. Within seconds, he rolled to an upright position with his legs tucked under his body. From this position he considered the world for the first time, shaking some of the last vestiges of birthing fluids from his eyes and ears.
>
> The mother giraffe lowered her head long enough to take a quick look. Then she repositioned herself so that she was standing directly over the calf. She waited for

about a minute and then did the most unreasonable thing. She swung her pendulous leg outward and kicked her baby, so that it was sent sprawling head over heels (or hooves, in this case). I turned to Jack and exclaimed, "Why'd she do that?"

"She wants it to get up, and if it doesn't she'll do it again."

Jack was right—the violent process was repeated again and then again. The struggle to rise was momentous, and as the baby grew tired of trying, the mother would again stimulate its efforts with a hearty kick.

Finally, amidst the cheers of the animal care staff, the calf stood for the first time. Wobbly, for sure, but it stood. Then we were struck silent when she kicked it off its feet again.

Jack's face was the only face not expressing astonishment. "She wants it to remember how it got up," he offered. "That's why she knocked it down. In the wild it would need to get up as soon as possible to follow the herd. The mother needs the herd, too. Lions, hyenas, leopards, and hunting dogs all would enjoy young giraffes. They'd get it, too, if the mother didn't teach her baby to quickly get up and get with it."[1]

What an example of the justice of God. In His dealings with men, He gives unbelievers a kick of conviction to make them see their need of salvation so that prowling Satan doesn't devour them. In His dealings with Christians, He gives us a kick by allowing stress to come into our lives so that we'll be strong in our ability to stand against Satan.

God's justice is not always clearly evident. At times our hearts cry out with David, "For I was envious of the arrogant, as I saw the prosperity of the wicked. For there are no pains in their death; and their body is fat. They are not in trouble as other men; nor are they plagued like mankind" (Ps. 73:3-5).

But after thinking about it, David concludes, "When I pondered to understand this, it was troublesome in my sight until I came into the sanctuary of God; then I perceived their end" (vv. 16-17).

David resolved his mental conflict by coming into the presence of God, being reminded again of God's faithful attributes, such as His justice.

J. I. Packer's thoughts are similar.

> God has resolved to be every man's Judge, rewarding every man according to his works. Retribution is the inescapable moral law of creation; God will see that each man sooner or later receives what he deserves—if not here, then hereafter. . . . the character of God is the guarantee that all wrongs will be righted some day; when "the day of wrath and revelation of the righteous judgement of God" (Romans 2:5) arrives, retribution will be exact, and no problems of cosmic unfairness will remain to haunt us. God is the Judge, so justice will be done.[2]

This is a comforting thought for any Christian who has witnessed the absence of fairness in our world. As Christians, we are assured that God will be just in evaluating our lives. The advantage we have is that our sins are cleansed by the blood of Jesus. God's wrath—His justice toward those without Jesus—will not be leveled against us.

Another element of God's justice is that He does not require what we are unable to give. John Bisagno relates, "Our God is generous as well as benevolent. He exhibits lovingkindness as well as understanding. He does not demand what we are incapable of giving, but instead He gives us what we are incapable of finding on our own."[3]

I will feel grateful when I stand before the Almighty God of justice. I won't be afraid, knowing He'll judge fairly. Since I'll be clothed in Jesus' righteousness, God's judgment and wrath will not be leveled toward me. I'll only experience His compassion and forgiveness.

––––––––

God of justice, I exalt You for Your fair dealings with mankind. You've made the way of escape available through Jesus and brought me down the narrow path into eternal life. Amen.

23 / God Is Immutable

Something that is immutable is something that never changes. With God, there is no possibility that He will ever be altered in any way.

"For I am the Lord, I change not" (Mal. 3:6, KJV).

Imagine that you have some bad news to tell your spouse. You're feeling uptight and anxious, wondering how he or she will respond. As you contemplate the situation, you think, Well, now, I remember one time I told him something similar, and he blew up. He was furious. Oh, no, he's probably going to respond that way again. But wait a minute . . . I remember another time I told him something like this, and he acted as if it were no big deal. He laughed it off and told me to forget it. See? That's not so bad. Hmmm, I wonder which way he's going to act this time?

We need never feel that way about God, because He never changes. He is faithful to respond as He always has, and He will not alter His viewpoint or His perspective. That would be against His nature. That is impossible!

Mullins says:

> We might sum up the meaning of God's immutability by saying, it is His moral personal self-consistency in all His dealings with His creatures. The tune of a simple song like "Home, Sweet Home" may be played on an instrument with variations. But through all variations the tune runs in self-consistent unity to the end. God's immutability is like the tune. It is His self-consistency manifesting itself in endless variations of method.[1]

But aren't there examples in the Bible where God changed His mind, as in the Book of Jonah, where He decided not to bring judgment upon Nineveh? Broche explains:

> A boat rows against the stream; the current resists it. So is a nation violating the law of God; it is subject to judgment. The boat turns and goes with the stream, the current assists it. So is a nation which has repented and put itself into harmony with God's law; it is subject to a blessing. But the current is the same; it has not changed,

only the boat has changed its relationship to the current. Neither does God change—we change; and the same law which executed itself in punishment now expresses itself in blessing.[2]

Since our world and the people around us, including ourselves, change, grow, improve, or deteriorate, we view God's immutability with wonder. And yet His changelessness cannot be any other way. If God were to improve, that would mean He wasn't already perfect—and He *is* perfect. If God were to decline in any of His qualities, then He would be capable of being less than who He is. Impossible! God does not change. He has no need to change. He is already everything, complete to the fullest, and He will never fail to live up to that perfection.

What does all this mean to us? A. W. Tozer gives us the answer so beautifully.

> In this world where men forget us, change their attitude toward us as their private interests dictate, and revise their opinion of us for the slightest cause, is it not a source of wondrous strength to know that the God with whom we have to do changes not? That His attitude toward us now is the same as it was in eternity past and will be in eternity to come?
>
> What peace it brings to the Christian's heart to realize that our Heavenly Father never differs from Himself. In coming to Him at any time we need not wonder whether we shall find Him in a receptive mood. He is always receptive to misery and need, as well as to love and faith. He does not keep office hours nor set aside periods when He will see no one. Neither does He change His mind about anything. Today, this moment, He feels toward His creatures, toward babies, toward the sick, the fallen, the sinful, exactly as He did when He sent His only-begotten Son into the world to die for mankind.[3]

Immutable God, thank You for Your consistent nature. I can rest assured that You will respond to me with love, always wanting what's best for me. At times I may interpret Your actions as being inconsistent, but by faith I believe You are the same and look at me the same. Amen.

24 / God Is Gentle

God demonstrates His gentleness by His tenderness toward us. He is understanding and touches our lives with kindness and love.

"Now, I, Paul, myself urge you by the meekness and gentleness of Christ—I who am meek when face to face with you, but bold toward you when absent!" (2 Cor. 10:1).

Jack Badal tells this story of how he was chosen to become the trainer for the Los Angeles Zoo.

They brought the three of us candidates into a waiting room and told us to please sit down. Animal trainers are a funny breed, and we didn't talk much while we were waiting for our turn to be interviewed. They called the first guy in and about two minutes later we heard a macaw squawking his head off. In another two minutes the first guy comes out. He's red-faced and doesn't say a word. He just leaves in a huff. The second guy goes in and the same thing happens again, only the bird is even louder than before. Number two comes out shaking his head, looks at me, rolls his eyes, and leaves. I wondered what was going on.

"Mr. Badal, would you please come in?" asked one of the interviewers. I said, "Yes, sir," and walked right into the room. There were some important men from city hall, and the zoo directors, of course. Right in the middle of the room was a large cage with a very nervous scarlet macaw. He was looking at everybody and rocking back and forth because he was still upset.

The director said, "So you want to be our trainer, Mr. Badal?"

"Yes, sir," I answered.

"We would like to get a little idea of your skills, Mr. Badal." They handed me a small bird net with about a two-foot handle and asked me if I would please take the macaw out of the cage for them.

I knew just what had been happening. The two guys ahead of me were manhandling the bird. They had most likely netted the bird, drug him out of the cage, and put him back in. That's why the bird was so upset. I hid the net behind my back and spoke quietly to the bird until I could see that he was calming down. Then I slowly and carefully opened the door and let him get used to that. I turned the net around and offered the handle to the bird. He stepped right on and I lifted him out of the cage slowly and stood before the interview board.

I said, "Now what would you like me to do with the bird?"

"Put him back in the cage, Mr. Badal. And congratulations—you are our new trainer."[1]

Do you feel like you've been manhandled by life and you're wondering whether God is really gentle? Let me assure you, God *is* gentle. When we feel raw and wounded, it may not seem like it, but He is. He never changes. Our circumstances change. People hurt us. Cars break down. Friends misunderstand us. But God is gentle and kind.

God is reaching out to you, not with a net, but with a handle. Hold on.

Gentle Lord, I confess that at times I wonder whether You truly are gentle. It's hard to understand why difficult circumstances are allowed in my life. But by faith, I'll choose to believe that You are gentle. Amen.

25 / God Is Available

When we say God is available, we mean He is present, attentive, and dependable when needed.

"God is our refuge and strength, a very present help in trouble. Therefore we will not fear" (Ps. 46:1-2).

I was looking forward to having my monthly morning in prayer at our local regional park. Knowing I would need $1.50 to get in, I was proud of myself for coming prepared with the six quarters. Driving into the entrance of the park, I rolled down my window, leaned out, and deposited the money into the machine. I glanced to the front of me, expecting to see the mechanical arm going up. I stared ahead in shock and surprise. There wasn't any arm at all!

Wait a minute! I put in my six quarters for nothing! If only I'd looked first, I could have gotten in free! I drove into the park, vowing to never again assume the arm was there. (It *was* there every time after that!)

Thinking later about that experience, I mused how we as Christians try to use good works to gain God's availability. We drop in our quarters:

Lord, I did my Bible reading today. Aren't I a good girl? Will You listen to my prayers now?

Jesus, I've prayed every day this week. Now will You say yes to my request?

Spirit, I've been submitting to my unbelieving husband. Now will You hear my plea to convict him and get him saved? Please!

While we're putting in all these quarters, thinking God is more pleased with us, His arms have been open to receive us all along. His availability has nothing to do with our performance.

Maybe you've been away from the Lord, and you want to receive His forgiveness; but something inside you says, "I must clean up my act first before I can have access to God."

Don't put in the quarters! God has already opened His arms to you through His Son, Jesus. Just walk in and know His love, forgiveness, and cleansing are yours for the taking—not for the paying. Then do good works, not because you're earning God's availability, but because He's empowering you to fulfill His plan for you.

———

Awesome Lord, it's incredible to me that the Almighty God is available to me at any moment without having to pay anything. I come to You now in faith, knowing nothing stands in the way of Your unconditional love and acceptance. Amen.

26 / God Is Wrathful

God has the ability to become angry, yet His anger is always righteous indignation toward sin.

"For the wrath of God is revealed from heaven against all ungodliness and unrighteousness of men" (Rom. 1:18).

It's hard to think of the wrath of God. It's even harder to consider it as a quality of God. We'd much rather think about His love, compassion, faithfulness—anything that will give us good, comfortable feelings. Yet we must honestly acknowledge His wrath as a part of who He is.

Maybe it's hard for us to think of God's wrath because when we think of anger, we envision man's out-of-control kind of anger. We think of how we are when we're angry: we feel helpless, confused, hurt, revengeful, and lacking in self-control. At times, these feelings give birth to hitting, spanking in anger, violence, rage, even murder. Surely all that can't describe God.

And that's exactly the point. Our image of man's wrath is not the way God expresses His wrath. His mind doesn't go blank. He doesn't hit in fury. He doesn't yell because He feels helpless and ignored. We do; He doesn't.

J. I. Packer says, "God's wrath in the Bible is never the capricious, self-indulgent, irritable, morally ignoble thing that human anger so often is. It is, instead, a right and necessary reaction to objective moral evil. God is only angry where anger is called for. Even among men, there is such a thing as *righteous* indignation, though it is, perhaps, rarely found. But all God's indignation is righteous."[1]

We were made in the image of God; and just as He experiences anger and wrath, you and I experience it also. In my book *Healing the Angry Heart*, I talk about how God put that characteristic in our lives because He wanted us to be motivated to correct wrongs. He wanted us to become energized to fight injustice. I cringe when I find in myself a great deal of apathy toward injustice unless I get angry about it. Then I have energy and motivation. Unfortunately, since our anger is seldom pure "righteous indignation," our anger often gets expressed in destructive, unfair methods. Actually, God intended for that energy to be used constructively toward righting wrongs.

I recently received a fund-raising letter from a Christian organization, and the first sentence said, "This letter is going to make you angry." I thought, What an interesting, direct way to grab the readers' attention and to let them know the emotion the writer wishes the readers to experience. Several times throughout the letter, it said the readers should get angry so that they would respond to the evil the organization was fighting.

I also thought it was interesting that fund-raising must be addressed in such a manner, possibly indicating that Christians aren't easily motivated to address and fight evil.

That's not the case with God. He is constantly fighting evil and sin, not with out-of-control hitting, but with His ever-ready willingness to bring judgment and justice into this world.

David Needham writes:

> To begin with, we must know—if we are ever to know God—something of the intensity of His wrath. His scathing, reverberating repulsion toward everything that is contrary to holiness. Sin must not go unpunished regardless of who has to suffer. In fact, one of sin's most hideous characteristics is that so often its painful effects spread far beyond the individual who commits the sin. Punishment is God's absolute, unbending edict. We might wish this were not so. That He would simply cancel the consequences, forgive and forget.[2]

But He cannot do that. He does, though, offer a way out of the consequences of sin through the gracious gift of salvation through Jesus Christ. But if a man chooses to refuse that invitation to eternal life, God gives man only what he desires—and deserves.

"The unbeliever has preferred to be by himself, without God, defying God, having God against him, and he shall have his preference. Nobody stands under the wrath of God save those who have chosen to do so. The essence of God's action in wrath is to *give men what they choose,* in all its implications: nothing more, and equally nothing less."[3]

It helps me understand this characteristic when I think of my role as a parent. When my children disobey and I discipline them, my goal is that they make the right choice the next time. I'm not giving them a consequence because I want to hurt them, but because I know they need something to remind them to correct their actions.

God's wrath, likewise, is intended to turn people from their evil and to prevent the evil from spreading. God hates evil and its horrible consequences; therefore His wrath is exhibited toward anyone and everything that violates His plan for goodness and righteousness. If it weren't for the robe of Jesus' righteousness that you and I are wearing, we would be in that category.

———————

Holy God, You do feel wrath about the injustice and evil filling our world. And I'm glad because otherwise I'd feel very helpless in fighting it myself. You are responding to it, and one day all evil will be gone, replaced by a new heaven and a new earth filled with Your righteousness. Amen.

27 / God Is Jealous

God's jealousy is righteous, based on His wanting His people to stay true to Him.

"You shall not worship them or serve them; for I, the Lord your God, am a jealous God" (Exod. 20:5).

Like the wrath of God, it seems wrong calling God a jealous God. We recall the destructiveness of a husband or wife's jealousy that can ruin a marriage. Their jealousy (whether based on fact or not) becomes an all-consuming passion, as insecurity and suspicion fuel their imagination.

But this is not a portrayal of God's jealousy. When the Bible describes God's jealousy, it is speaking anthropomorphically. J. I. Packer explains that scientific word *anthropomorphisms* as descriptions of God in language drawn from the life of man. . . . The reason why God uses these terms to speak to us about Himself is that language drawn from our own personal life is the most accurate medium for communicating thoughts about Him that we have. . . .

. . . God's jealousy is not a compound of frustration, envy, and spite, as human jealousy so often is, but appears instead as a (literally) praiseworthy zeal to preserve something supremely precious.[1]

That precious relationship with God is often described in the Bible as a kind of marriage relationship. And what husband or wife, knowing of the unfaithfulness of his or her spouse, would not have a righteous jealousy, desiring to see the sanctity of their marriage kept intact?

Although we humans don't always handle such situations with righteousness, God does. His reactions are meant to draw the beloved back into a pure relationship with Him. Much of Moses' writing (and the rest of the Old Testament) speaks of this longing of God to draw the Israelites back into a love relationship. Packer comments, "From these passages we see plainly what God meant by telling Moses that His name was 'Jealous.' He meant that He demands from those whom He has loved and redeemed utter and absolute loyalty, and will vindicate His claim by stern action against them if they betray His love by unfaithfulness."[2] God calls out to His Bride, the Church, and says, "Reject your lovers called materialism and worldliness, and come back to be faithful to Me. I love you."

In the Old Testament Book of Hosea, the prophet pleads with his unfaithful wife, Gomer, to return to their marriage. This is God's illustration of how He faithfully seeks His bride, the Israelites, wanting them to worship only Him. Hosea is a beautiful example of God's unconditional love. He never stops loving, yet He still expresses His disapproval and executes discipline.

That's a description of God's jealousy. He desires our faithfulness in worshiping and obeying Him. When we do not, His love will discipline us because He wants us to turn back to true commitment to Him.

When we worship the gods of materialism or worldliness, we are bowing before other gods and giving them glory and praise. That is against the "marriage vows" we've taken with God to serve only Him. God says, "I am the Lord, that is My name; I will not give My glory to another, nor My praise to graven images" (Isa. 42:8).

Packer writes, "God seeks what we should seek—His glory, in and through men—and it is for the securing of this end, ultimately, that He is jealous. His jealousy, in all its manifestations, is precisely 'the zeal of the LORD of hosts' . . . for fulfilling His own purpose of justice and mercy."[3]

May we desire that also.

Jealous God, may everything that has breath acknowledge Your supremacy and give glory to Your name. I worship You and commit again to casting out any idols in my life that could make You jealous. Amen.

28 / God Is Self-sufficient

God is complete within himself. He needs nothing, nor does He use anything outside himself.

"For just as the Father has life in Himself, even so He gave to the Son also to have life in Himself" (John 5:26).

We are very needy people. We need companionship, food, shelter, water, a relationship with God—and many, many other things that could more accurately come under the column "Wants." I cannot imagine what it would be like to not need anything.

Yet, God doesn't need anything. He is completely fulfilled in himself. He didn't need to create the world. He didn't need to have the fellowship of His creatures, mankind. He didn't need to have Jesus come to earth. He did not create the universe or provide for salvation out of any need of His own. None of those things fulfill Him or expand Him or perfect Him. He is already the fullest of what He is or can be. There's nothing that can be added to Him.

Dick Eastman writes:

> Because every living organism depends on circumstances or situations outside of itself that affect its existence, it is virtually impossible to conceive of anything functioning independently. Yet, this is the case with God. Pope writes, "No notion we can form of God is more important in its meaning than that He is self-sufficient. All things have their cause and their end in Him. He is the one, sole, self-originated, independent, unconditioned and absolute Being . . . God simply, purely, eternally IS! He is a being who needs nothing to complement or complete His perfection . . . His self-sufficiency knows no limit but what He himself by word or act assigns to it."[1]

Unfortunately, because of our human viewpoint, the truth of this quality of God is hard for us to grasp. We somehow believe that because He made us, He must have needed our conversation so that He wouldn't be lonely. We think God needs our help. We think God can't fulfill His plan without us assisting Him. Surely He must need our backing to make His gospel message known throughout the world.

Yes, God has chosen to enjoy our fellowship, but He doesn't "need" us. Yes, God has chosen to use us in spreading the gospel, but He doesn't "need" our help. He is completely content with His own company, and He is thoroughly capable of making the message known without us.

A. W. Tozer writes some strong words to this effect.

> Probably the hardest thought of all for our natural egotism to entertain is that God does not need our help. We commonly represent Him as a busy, eager, somewhat frustrated Father hurrying about seeking help to carry out His benevolent plan to bring peace and salvation to the world. . . .
>
> Too many missionary appeals are based upon this fancied frustration of Almighty God. An effective speaker can easily excite pity in his hearers, not only for the hea-

then but for the God who has tried so hard and so long to save them and has failed for want of support. I fear that thousands of young persons enter Christian service from no higher motive than to help deliver God from the embarrassing situation His love has gotten Him into and His limited abilities seem unable to get Him out of. . . .

Let us not imagine that the truth of the divine self-sufficiency will paralyze Christian activity. Rather it will stimulate all holy endeavor. This truth, while a needed rebuke to human self-confidence, will when viewed in its Biblical perspective lift from our minds the exhausting load of mortality and encourage us to take the easy yoke of Christ and spend ourselves in Spirit-inspired toil for the honor of God and the good of mankind. For the blessed news is that the God who needs no one has in sovereign condescension stooped to work by and in and through His obedient children.[2]

This is good news! God doesn't need anyone or anything, yet He wants to use us. This thought should make us feel even more loved and important. For God doesn't desire our fellowship and our activity out of some unhealthy, sick need; He desires us because He enjoys us. He doesn't *have to,* He *wants to.* If He wanted our company because of some dysfunctional need, we might not feel so loved. But the fact that He desires it because He enjoys it can make us feel important.

Should we call upon Him because it fulfills a need within Him? No! But because He desires to help us. This will bring Him honor. But even for Him to be honored, we are not necessary, for the Bible says that even if we don't praise Him, the rocks will. God doesn't even *need* praise. He knows who He is, and that's enough.

One of the mothers in my parenting class told me this story: She was wondering whether her son was embarrassed by her walking him to kindergarten each day. When she asked him if he wanted her to go with him, he replied, "It's OK, Mom. You can come as long as you need to."

Praise the Lord. God doesn't need us, but He wants us.

———

Self-sufficient Father, although my mind can't comprehend some-

*one who doesn't need anything outside himself, I thank You that
You desire my company and fellowship. Amen.*

29 / God Is God

"For I am God, and there is no other; I am God, and there is no
one like Me" (Isa. 46:9).

Now that we've come to the end of this section and have
examined some of the qualities of God, I hope you can join me
in praising God for who He is. The best way to appreciate His
personhood is to say, "God is God." All these wonderful, awesome qualities are wrapped up in that three-lettered English
word *God*. We can say it quickly and without much effort, and
yet the impact it carries is beyond our ability to completely comprehend.

I hope our study has made you more desirous of praising
God and appreciating His qualities—causing Him to be manifest
in your thinking as an awe-inspiring God and yet a personal,
loving God interested in every aspect of your life.

This is not the end of learning about God; it's only the beginning. A wonderful thing about our study of God is that it
need never end. Near the end of a good book have you ever
thought, Even though I want to find out the conclusion, I don't
want the book to end because I'm enjoying this so much?

We never need to feel like that about our study and growth
in knowing God. It's something that we can do for the rest of our
days, until our very last moment of consciousness.

I pray that Moses' request of God in Exod. 33:13 (Amp.)
will be your prayer: "Now, therefore, I pray You, if I have found
favor in Your sight, show me now Your way, that I may know
You [progressively become more deeply and intimately ac-
quainted with You, perceiving and recognizing and understand-

ing more strongly and clearly] that I may find favor in Your sight."

The knowledge of God is like a treasure that is constantly being revealed more and more. Some people are close to discovering Him but don't even realize it. They go through life without ever having experienced the ultimate joy of knowing Him.

In 1985 Mel Fisher found a Spanish galleon that had been sunk in 1622 by a hurricane off the Straits of Florida. After searching for this ship for 16 years, Mel and his crew finally found their treasure. It was worth $400 million.

When the galleon was discovered, not only was its ancient gold and silver uncovered, but also were more familiar objects—like monofilament line and sinkers. It turns out that fishermen had sat above the treasure for years, but all they were looking for was fish, when a vast treasure was there for the taking.

———

Lord God, I worship You. I worship the great God that You are. Although I can never know all of You, I thank You that You've given me a peek at Your greatness and depth. I want to know You more and more. Thank You that You want to be known. Amen.

SECTION II

God's View of You

30 / God Views You as Having Grace

Grace is that undeserved love and favor God offers us, even though He knows we can never deserve it, earn it, or repay Him for it.

"For by grace you have been saved through faith; and that not of yourselves, it is the gift of God" (Eph. 2:8).

"He saved us, not on the basis of deeds which we have done in righteousness, but according to His mercy, by the washing of regeneration and renewing by the Holy Spirit" (Titus 3:5).

Larry and I were excited for Rick and Fausta as we attended their wedding. At the sit-down dinner later, we looked across the filled room, marveling at Fausta's many relatives.

When it was time to leave, Larry and I went up to the newlyweds. "We wish you the very best," Larry said, shaking Rick's hand and giving Fausta a peck on her cheek.

I grinned and said, "The wedding was gorgeous, and the reception was incredible. Thank you for a wonderful time."

Rick and Fausta accepted our greetings with a smile. Then Fausta said, "Kathy, wait just a moment. I have a gift for you."

Fausta turned and walked away. I stood there dumbfounded. Wait a minute, I thought. I brought Fausta a gift. She's not supposed to give me a gift.

I turned to Larry with a questioning look, but he returned my gaze as if to say, "Don't look at me. I don't know what's going on."

Within moments, Fausta returned. In her hand she had a white box four or five inches square with a delicate white ribbon wrapped around it. As she offered me the gift, I wanted to say, "Fausta, I can't take this from you. I brought *you* a gift; you're not supposed to give *me* a gift. It's your wedding, not mine!"

Instead, I reached out my hand, took the box, and said, "Fausta, that's so sweet of you. Thank you very much."

As we drove home, I began to untie the ribbon. Then I discovered a small silver seal glued to the bottom of the box. It said, "Made in Milan, Italy."

I gasped. "Oh, Larry. This must be expensive. It says it's made in Italy. Why did she give me this gift?"

I quickly pulled the top off, peeled away the layer of tissue paper, and stared at a beautiful sterling silver candy dish. "Look, Larry. Isn't it beautiful?"

Larry nodded as I turned it over and over, studying its beauty. Then I noticed engraving in the center of the dish. "Larry, the letters *F* and *R* are engraved in the center, to remind me they gave it to me."

"That's really beautiful!" Larry exclaimed.

Then a wonderful thought dawned on me. "Larry, this dish could symbolize the gift of salvation God gives you and me. Just as I didn't do anything to deserve or earn this dish, so God offered the gift of His love and of being His child, even though I couldn't do anything to earn or deserve it. Isn't that just like His grace?"

Larry's smile confirmed he knew exactly what I was talking about, especially since he had introduced me to God's gift so many years earlier.

Now when I look at the silver dish, I'm gently reminded of God's wonderful gift of grace: something I never could have been good enough to earn or deserve.

Thank You, Heavenly Father, that in Your wisdom You knew I could never be good enough to measure up to Your perfect standard. That's why You sent Your Son Jesus to purchase my salvation. I'm so glad Your gift of grace is mine. Amen.

31 / God Views You as Strong

As a part of our inheritance, God gives us His strength: the ability to do that which we wouldn't be able to do on our own.

"I can do all things through Him who strengthens me" (Phil. 4:13).

Some time ago, a friend mentioned she'd slammed her finger in the car door and had to drill a hole in her fingernail to relieve the pressure and pain. I thought, I could never do that. It sounds like the most barbaric thing anyone could do. You won't catch me doing something horrible like that. Besides, I'm never going to have to face such a decision because I'm never going to slam my finger in the car door!

I had avoided that particular horror for the first 40 years of my life, and I planned to avoid it for the next 40, so that settled that—until two weeks later. I was rushing for a speaking engagement, had gotten into the car, and then remembered something else I needed. Getting out, I pushed the car door closed with the fingers of my right hand wrapped around the edge. Almost in slow motion as the door slammed on my hand, I thought, I don't think I'm supposed to leave my hand there. Crunch! Ouch!

Pain shot through my hand and up my arm. Quickly opening the door with my left hand, I pulled away my throbbing hand. The middle finger hurt the most. It ached so badly! I didn't have time to put ice on it but drove to my speaking engagement and was able to put the pain aside enough to speak.

The rest of the day, my swollen, black-and-blue finger throbbed with pain. When I complained to Larry about the aching, he said, "You may have to drill a hole in your nail."

I shot a look of horror at him. How dare he mention that terrible act! I'd said two weeks before I wouldn't do it, and I wasn't about to now. I could just imagine Larry holding his whirring drill against my nail and drilling a quarter-inch hole as blood spurted.

No way! That wasn't going to happen to me. I would suffer through the pain.

That night, my pulsating finger woke me up in the middle of the night. I swallowed two aspirin, but they didn't help the pain one bit.

By the next morning, I was desperate. The pain hadn't subsided at all. What was I going to do? How long was this going to continue? There must be a solution: but no, not the drill.

"Larry, I can't stand this pain. Even more aspirin doesn't help," I whined.

"Well, Kathy, I told you, drill a hole in your nail. Someone told me it didn't even hurt when they did it."

"Oh, yeah, sure. Doesn't hurt? How can that be? That's crazy!"

Larry looked back at me with a look of, "Well, you asked me what to do, and I told you; so don't expect anything more."

I held my right hand with my left, looking down at my blackened fingertip, which pulsated with my every heartbeat. *O Lord*, I prayed, *please help me. I can't stand this anymore!*

Before He could answer, I shouted to Larry, "OK! OK! What should I do?"

"Just a minute." Larry went into the garage and came back holding the smallest drill bit I'd ever seen. I took it in my trembling left hand, sat at my desk, and placed the tip of the drill bit against my nail. A shudder went through my body as I began twisting the drill bit against my nail. I continued to twist and turn it, any moment expecting tremendous pain and blood gushing from the nail.

Several times the drill bit slipped off my nail, and I jumped, I was so tense. I muttered a fast, *Help me, Lord!* and pressed the bit against my nail again. As the seconds passed, I looked at my nail and couldn't see any difference. But then, I noticed a small indentation in the nail. The drill bit didn't slip off center as much as before as I twisted it back and forth.

Any moment, it's going to go through the nail and hit the nail bed, and it's going to be extremely painful, I reminded myself with a grimace. But I was committed. I had to continue. The present pain wouldn't let me give up, even if it meant more pain.

And then about two or three minutes after starting, I lifted the bit and noticed the slightest bit of red liquid at the base of the indentation. Now for sure the pain is going to get worse. Again asking for God's help to continue, I resumed twisting the drill bit.

Fifteen seconds later, a bit of red blood seeped out, and I put the drill bit down. Blood now dribbled out of the hole, not spurting at all like I'd expected. I carefully and slowly squeezed the tip of my finger, and blood seeped out a little more. It didn't hurt to do that. It didn't hurt!

Wait a minute. It doesn't hurt at all anymore! The throbbing is gone.

"Larry!" I exclaimed. "It doesn't hurt anymore, and it didn't even hurt to drill the hole. I can't believe it!"

Larry smiled a knowing smile. "See?"

I stared at my finger, more blood oozing out as I squeezed it. It felt so good to have the pressure gone. I was relieved. It was over. *Thank You, Lord!*

Now, several months later, I'm still amazed that I had the strength to drill that hole in my nail.

What impossible situation are you facing where it is difficult for you to take action or to obey God? You need God's strength, and it's included in your inheritance as His child.

In order to lay hold of the strength He promises, take just 1 step toward the action He wants you to take. Don't worry about the other 10 steps you think you'll have to take; just take the first one. That's all He wants you to do. He'll supply the additional strength you need for steps 2, 3, and all the rest.

Consider that this difficult process may not actually be as painful as you expect, just like drilling into my nail. Remind yourself that even if the process is painful, the end result will help relieve your present pain, and that makes it worth it!

By the way, I ended up losing the nail of my middle finger, but the nail that has grown back is stronger than any of my other nails. Maybe you're going to have even more strength once you take that first step toward obeying God.

———

Precious Lord, thank You for the promise of Your strength right when I need it. Help me to trust that maybe the action You want me to take won't be as painful as it appears. Amen.

32 / God Views You as Having the Mind of Christ

God has made His children as new creatures. We view life differently than before because our mind is renewed through the indwelling Holy Spirit.

"For who has known the mind of the Lord, that he should instruct Him? But we have the mind of Christ" (1 Cor. 2:16).

Two years after becoming a new creature in Christ, I went to Jamaica as a short-term missionary for the summer. I was chosen to be in charge of two other girls, and we were one team among five located in Montego Bay. The two girls on my team had been Christians much longer than I, although they were younger in age. I felt intimidated by their seemingly greater knowledge. I wondered why I'd been chosen to be the captain.

One day I had to decide what we were going to do the next day. Most days were planned by our leaders, but this particular time I had full control over what my girls and I would do. I prayed and prayed. I asked the Lord for wisdom and knowledge of His leading. As a fairly new Christian, I hadn't heard God's voice before, but now I sought after the mind of Christ.

Finally, I sensed God wanting us to go to a nearby town to pass out tracts in an open-air market. Yes, that's what we would do. I knew I'd heard God's directions.

The next day, after we had breakfast and were preparing to leave, it started to rain. And then it poured! We usually went out in the rain, since it rained almost every afternoon in tropical Jamaica, but this was no usual light rain. It was coming down hard, and I knew no one would be in the uncovered market. I couldn't believe it. Hadn't God told me what to do? Now that it was raining, we wouldn't be able to go.

I was discouraged. I didn't really hear God's voice. What kind of a Christian am I that I can't learn to use the mind of Christ He's given me? My confidence hit bottom.

Looking back with more than 24 years' experience as a Christian, I have a much different perspective. I've learned through the years that having the mind of Christ doesn't necessarily mean we'll always know the right thing to do or that we'll always hear the leading of the Holy Spirit clearly.

God does promise to guide us, but it's a walk of faith, where guidance is sometimes a matter of stepping out into the dark and not being surprised if we fall off a cliff.

Unfortunately, we can get the idea that being led by the Holy Spirit means things like:

- I'll always know why things happen and why God is moving in a certain way.
- I should always be able to see a good result if God is leading.
- I should be able to control my circumstances and the evil in this world with my prayers (and that includes other people's actions and decisions).
- I won't ever make a mistake if I'm being led by God and walking in His will for me.
- When good things don't result from my good choices, it must mean I didn't make the right choice to begin with.

These faulty perceptions about living the Christian life bring discouragement, doubt, hurt, and even anger. We begin to question whether we ever had the wisdom of God or were being led by Him.

Regardless of these imperfections, God will indeed fulfill His purpose of glorifying himself and fulfilling His plan.

> For the truth is that God in His wisdom, to make and keep us humble and to teach us to walk by faith, has hidden from us almost everything that we should like to know about the providential purposes which He is working out in the churches and in our own lives. "As thou knowest not what is the way of the wind, nor how the bones do grow in the womb of her that is with child; even so thou knowest not the work of God who doeth all" (Eccles. 11:5, RV).[1]

Someone has said, "It doesn't matter how much money you have; everyone has to buy wisdom on the installment plan." Having the mind of Christ is also learned on the installment plan: little by little, with experience, and sometimes disappointment and hurt.

But the sweet fruit of wisdom does grow.

———————

Patient Lord, I claim my right to Christ's mind, but I also know I must grow into that right. I submit myself to Your school of wisdom and trust that You know the right way to teach me. Amen.

33 / God's View of You Is Peaceful

The more we learn to trust in God, the more we can take advantage of the peace God offers us.

"Peace I leave with you; My peace I give to you; not as the world gives, do I give to you. Let not your heart be troubled, nor let it be fearful" (John 14:27).

I was on the phone when Larry returned home from the doctor's office. After finishing my conversation, I went into the family room and sat down opposite him.

"What did the doctor say?" I eagerly questioned, fully expecting him to say, "Oh, he said there's no problem."

Instead, Larry looked straight in my eyes and replied, "It could be melanoma. Dr. Hanson's going to remove and biopsy the mole next Tuesday."

I smiled at him, even as I realized smiling was a crazy reaction to the deadly serious news he had just given me. Melanoma cancer: the deadliest kind of skin cancer! This just couldn't be happening. Larry and I would be celebrating our 41st birthdays and our 20th wedding anniversary later this month. He was too young to have something serious like this, and I was certainly too young to become a widow.

For the next 30 minutes, we sat and talked quietly. We remembered a friend who had died from melanoma. It seemed unbelievable that we could be facing the same war we'd seen Bob wage and lose only three years earlier.

The next day was Saturday. Tuesday seemed a long way off. I felt numb and yet strangely peaceful. God is in control, I reminded myself even as I prayed for Him to spare Larry's life. Larry also believed God knew what He was doing and trusted that He would do the right thing for him and our family.

Over the weekend, we alerted many people to pray, and the peace in our hearts continued to push away any sense of panic. My present reaction was so different from the time I discovered a lump in my left armpit. I shook my fist at God that time, telling Him He couldn't be a good God to let something like this happen to me. When it turned out to be nothing but a slight infection, I was truly grateful for God's mercy.

Now I didn't feel like shaking my fist at God. Although there were times when my tears fell and I grieved over possibly losing my wonderful husband, Larry and I continued to talk about our feelings. We drew closer to each other and to God than ever before. I was amazed at our reactions. God's peace really permeated our thinking. It was an incredible experience.

Only one night did worry keep me awake. I woke up at three in the morning and couldn't get back to sleep because of worrying whether Larry might die. As I lay there, my mind went back and forth between worry and trusting in God's will.

In my mind I recalled what I'd shared at a women's luncheon the previous afternoon. I'd given each of the ladies a 3" x 5" index card, and on one side I had them write in big letters, "STOP." For writing on the other side, I gave them several choices: Prov. 3:5-6; Isa. 26:3; Phil. 4:6-7; or Isa. 41:10. Picking one, they wrote out the verse.

Then I instructed them to carry the card with them; and whenever they recognized they were worrying, they were to pull out their card, say "STOP" out loud twice, turn the card over, and read out loud their verse. I assured them this little exercise would help them turn their attention and trust to the Lord.

Now as I lay in bed with worry choking out trust and peace, I knew I must use the same technique. I envisioned holding up the index card, shouted STOP in my mind twice, and then quoted Phil. 4:6-7. Worry scampered out of my mind as God's peace flooded it.

Yes, I could trust God's promise of peace to guard my heart and mind.

———————

Trustworthy Lord, I put my belief in Your ability to give me peace even when I can't conjure it up myself—especially when I can't conjure it up myself. Your peace is real. I praise You! Amen.

34 / God Views You as Justified

Justification is God declaring a believing sinner to be righteous and acceptable because of Jesus' death on the Cross.

"Therefore having been justified by faith, we have peace with God through our Lord Jesus Christ" (Rom. 5:1).

In July 1941, in the Auschwitz extermination camp, Sgt. Franciszek Gajowniczek was selected at random to be killed. Wanting to see his wife and children again, the condemned man pleaded for his life.

Suddenly a fellow prisoner, a Franciscan priest named Kolbe, stepped forward and offered to take the doomed man's place. He explained, "I am alone in this world and would be willing to die instead of this family man." The Nazis allowed the priest to take the sergeant's place; and a few weeks later, Rev. Kolbe died from starvation and a dose of carbolic acid.

Sgt. Gajowniczek survived Auschwitz and was reunited with his family at the end of the war. In 1972 he attended a ceremony at the barracks of Auschwitz to honor the man who had died in his place.

You and I are like Sgt. Gajowniczek—condemned to die because of the sins we've committed, having fallen short of God's holy standards.

But then, to our surprise, a man named Jesus volunteers to die in our place, even though He never sinned. Our hearts sink as we realize He is the Son of God. We don't deserve to have such a holy sacrifice. Yet, here He tells us for this very purpose He was born. With eyes looking at us in love and compassion, He spills His blood on Calvary's hill.

When we are justified, we take on the robe of Jesus' righteousness and become like His sinless nature in God's eyes. No longer do we wear the filthy robes of our sinfulness. Instead, we stand before God clothed in Jesus' perfection, "just as if we'd never sinned."

John Bisagno says it this way: "Volumes could be written on the theological aspects of justification, but it is, simply stated, that I stand complete in Him, clothed in righteousness, accepted in the Beloved as though I had never been what I was before."[1]

Heavenly Father, it's an awesome thought for me to realize that through Your sacrifice I stand forgiven and justified. Thank You that You've done for me what I could never have done myself. Amen.

35 / God Views You as Praying

It is awesome to think that we have the privilege of coming into the presence of the God of the Universe, and yet that's exactly what God wants us—longs for us—to do.

"Let us therefore draw near with confidence to the throne of grace, that we may receive mercy and may find grace to help in time of need" (Heb. 4:16).

When I walked into the church nursery on Sunday morning, Janet immediately said, "Kathy, I had a dream about you

Friday night. In it I was praying for you. I woke up and felt a tremendous burden to pray for you, so I did all yesterday. Is something going on in your life?"

I stared at Janet in wonder. The chance of Janet feeling led to pray for me when we only had contact twice a month was amazing to me.

"Janet, this is incredible. I am having a crisis. Larry found out on Friday that he's having a mole removed and biopsied this coming Tuesday. I really needed your prayers after hearing he could have melanoma."

Janet smiled even as a concerned look crossed her face. "I'm so glad I prayed for you. I've never dreamed about you before. I'll keep praying."

What a merciful God that He would speak to Janet's heart about praying for me. It demonstrated God's concern and care for Larry and me.

One of the incredible privileges we have as children of God is prayer. I'm amazed that I can enter boldly into the throne room of God and make my concerns known, and He actually cares and responds! That's even more amazing than walking up to the White House, telling the receptionist I want to speak to the president of the United States, and seeing her immediately open the door to the Oval Office. That most likely will never happen to me. Yet I can open the door to God anytime I turn my attention to Him—and He'll always listen and respond.

———

Lord, help me be constantly aware of the invisible communication lines constantly open between You and me. Thank You for the amazing privilege of talking personally with You. Amen.

36 / God Views You as Chosen

God chooses me to be His child, not because of my worthiness, but because His wonderful love wants to draw me into His family.

"Blessed be the God and Father of our Lord Jesus Christ, who has blessed us with every spiritual blessing in the heavenly places in Christ, just as He chose us in Him before the foundation of the world, that we should be holy and blameless before Him" (Eph. 1:3-4).

D. L. Moody recounted:

I have read of an artist who wanted to paint a picture of the Prodigal Son. He searched through the madhouses, and the poorhouses, and the prisons, to find a man wretched enough to represent the prodigal, but he could not find one. One day he was walking down the streets and met a man whom he thought would do. He told the poor beggar he could pay him well if he came to his room and sat for his portrait. The beggar agreed, and the day was appointed for him to come.

The day came, and a man put in his appearance at the artist's room. "You made an appointment with me," he said, when he was shown into the studio. The artist looked at him. "I never saw you before," he said. "You cannot have an appointment with me."

"Yes," he said, "I agreed to meet you today at 10 o'clock."

"You must be mistaken; it must have been some other artist; I was to see a beggar here at this hour."

"Well," says the beggar, "I am he."

"You?"

"Yes."

"Why, what have you been doing?"

"Well, I thought I would dress myself up a bit before I got painted."

"Then," said the artist, "I do not want you; I wanted you as you were; now you are no use to me."[1]

When God chose you and me to be His children, it was not

87

dependent on our getting cleaned up or making ourselves free of sin. He chose us based solely upon His unconditional love and acceptance of us, regardless of our sinful state. As Eph. 1:4 states, "He chose us in Him before the foundation of the world," not after we got our act together.

Gracious Lord, it's amazing to me that You would choose me, even though I'm not worthy of Your call upon my life. Help me to fully comprehend and experience the great love You have for me and for everyone. Amen.

37 / God Views You as Blessed

God makes available to His children every spiritual blessing so that they can grow, be equipped to serve, and respond in the Holy Spirit's power.

"Blessed be the God and Father of our Lord Jesus Christ, who has blessed us with every spiritual blessing in the heavenly places in Christ" (Eph. 1:3).

> There was an extremely wealthy man who possessed vast treasures of art. The man had one son who was an ordinary boy, and who passed away in late adolescence. Having loved the lad deeply, the sorrowing father died of a broken heart only a few weeks later.
>
> The father's will provided that everything would be sold by auction and strangely, the father stipulated that an oil painting of his son was to be the first item offered by the auctioneer. Large crowds came to bid on the widely reputed collection of art. In keeping with the proviso of the will, the boy's portrait was first held up for bids. No one cared about the deceased boy. Not until several moments had passed, did an old . . . servant, who had always loved the boy, place a 75-cent bid.
>
> The picture was at once sold to the [servant], there being no further bids registered. Then the dramatic mo-

ment came; the sale was stopped, as the will had further provided that anyone who loved the son enough to buy his portrait should receive everything in the father's house.[1]

The moment you and I accepted Jesus Christ as our Savior and Lord, thus showing our love for God's Son, we received the inheritance of every spiritual blessing we could ever need.

The apostle Peter wrote it this way: "Seeing that His divine power has granted to us everything pertaining to life and godliness, through the true knowledge of Him who called us by His own glory and excellence" (2 Pet. 1:3).

I don't believe that means we won't have trials, illness, difficulties, and stress. For after all, in his first letter, Peter writes, "Beloved, do not be surprised at the fiery ordeal among you, which comes upon you for your testing, as though some strange thing were happening to you" (4:12).

The spiritual blessings given to us don't mean we'll never experience problems or temptations, but they do mean we'll have the Lord's power to cope and respond the way He wants us to. Truly, that is as important and precious as a servant receiving all the inheritance of a wealthy man.

———

Generous Father, You have wisely provided everything I need to live the way that pleases You. Thank You for Your provision and insight. Amen.

38 / God Views You as Redeemed

To be redeemed means to be bought back. Redemption is the price paid to buy a slave out of his bondage.

"In Him we have redemption through His blood, the forgiveness of our trespasses, according to the riches of His grace" (Eph. 1:7).

Seated on the bunk in my prison cell, I rested my head in my hands. How did I end up here? I don't want to be here! What went wrong?

Regret swept over me. I never envisioned running around with those people would end me up here. I didn't want to hurt those people, but I was caught up in the violence. I didn't think we could get caught, so it seemed exciting to go along with the gang.

I lifted my head to view the dull gray walls and the dirty sink across the room only a few feet away. If only I could go back in time, I'd make better choices.

Later at lunch, the prisoner sitting across from me drawled between his mouthfuls of meatloaf, "There's a rumor going around that some man is willing to take anyone's place in here for the rest of his sentence."

My mouth dropped open with disbelief. "You can't be serious. Who would want to come in here and stay voluntarily?"

"I don't know," he replied, "but that's what I heard." He shoved a spoonful of applesauce into his mouth. "It sounded too good to be true, so I just didn't believe it."

The man sitting next to me said, "Yeah, man, there must be some catch. Besides, I'm still maintaining my innocence, so if I let someone take my place, they might think I'm admitting I robbed that little old lady. I'm not falling for this; it must be some new trick to get me to admit I did the crime."

I'd heard of this man's crime and had concluded he was indeed guilty.

I looked across the table to a third man and asked his opinion of the rumor. "Well, I'm almost done with my sentence, and I figure since I did the crime, I'm gonna do the time." He shoveled a forkful of mashed potatoes into his mouth and continued, "That way when I get outa here, I can pat myself on the back that I did it m'self. I'm not gonna let nobody take that away from me."

I couldn't quite understand his thinking but didn't want to argue. I turned to a fourth man, who sat beside me on the left, and raised my eyebrows, indicating I wanted his opinion.

"Me?" He leaned closer and whispered in my ear. "Don't tell no one, but my old woman is setting up an escape plan for me. I should hear about it soon." With a grin that showed several missing teeth, he continued for everyone to hear, "So you can tell I don't need no other help."

I'd heard of this man's other unsuccessful escape attempts and knew I wanted no part of his ideas.

I stared at the first man and asked, "Do you have any idea how to look into that man's offer?"

Everyone at the table laughed or choked on their food as they looked at me with grins that told me I was foolish.

"Don't mind them, they're stupid anyway," the first man replied. "Well, like I said, it's only a rumor; but you could talk to the warden if you want. But I wouldn't get my hopes up if I were you."

"Thanks," I replied.

Several days later, after requesting to talk with the warden, the meeting time finally arrived. Walking into the warden's office, I tried to quiet my racing heart while wiping the sweat off my palms. In a crisp, businesslike way, the warden asked, "What do you want?"

With a trembling voice I replied, "I heard a rumor saying some man is willing to take the place of one of the inmates here. I didn't believe it, but I thought I'd ask anyway."

I started to rise from my seat, fully expecting the warden to laugh me out of his office, so I figured I might as well get a fast start.

"Yes, as a matter of fact, that is available. We don't understand why this is happening, but there is indeed an offer by some local worker to serve any inmate's term."

I fell back into my seat and stared incredulously at the warden. "What do I have to do to take advantage of this?"

The warden laughed slightly. "Well, that's the really weird part. This man only requires the inmate to admit his crime and believe he will actually come to take your place. Sounds outrageous, doesn't it?"

"Yeah, I'd expect him to at least want me to pay him some money or something."

"I would, too, but that's not it at all."

"Well, I want to do it. Will you let him know I've acknowledged my part in the crime and want him to take my place here?"

"I will indeed. You'll hear from us soon."

Walking back to my cell, I could hardly believe what had just transpired. Can it really be true that I'm about to be set free? The next day, the dream became a reality when a guard led me from my cell, taking me through the releasing process. As I signed my name to the release form, I could see a man being taken through the adjoining room, but he didn't look like a criminal at all. "Who is that?" I questioned.

The guard replied, "That's the man who's taking your place."

I stared at him, and as I did, he looked over at me. I silently mouthed, "Why?" He smiled back with a look of compassion in his eyes and said, "Because I love you." It was only then that I noticed the blood dripping from the palms of his hands.

––––––––––

Redeemer God, thank You for sending Your Son Jesus to take my place and buy my release from the bondage of sin. I accept Your love for me, even though I'm not worthy of it. I'm free to live now in the power of Your righteousness. Amen.

39 / God Views You as Important

God looks at His children as having value. One person would have been sufficient reason for Him to send His Son Jesus to this earth to die. It is not the number of people that makes us important. Just one individual is significant.

"Knowing that you were not redeemed with perishable things like silver or gold from your futile way of life inherited from your forefathers, but with precious blood, as of a lamb unblemished and spotless, the blood of Christ" (1 Pet. 1:18-19).

If you and I had not been important and valuable to God, He would not have been willing to sacrifice such a significant Person. But He was willing and did indeed give the life of His Son Jesus, the most important thing He could ever have forfeited.

We sometimes have a hard time regarding ourselves as important. Maybe we can relate to the status that a penny has in our society. The last time you noticed a penny on the street, did you pick it up? Few of us do. After all, we can't buy anything with it; and as they accumulate in our purse, wallet, or pocket, they only weigh us down.

Our attitude toward pennies is sometimes the way we view ourselves. "It's amazing to me that God would care enough about me to send Jesus just for me." "I'm not important enough for God to have put Jesus on the Cross." We feel like a single penny being run over on the street. Yet each of us is important, and joined with others we can make a powerful impact.

That fact was expressed in an Ann Landers column on August 10, 1989. "D. S." from the Baptist Home for Children in Bethesda, Md., wrote Ann, saying:

> A group of fund-raisers for our Baptist Children's Home was looking for a novel and painless way to raise funds. Someone figured out that 16 pennies equal one foot. Since there are 5,280 feet in a mile, a mile of pennies would equal $844.80. We launched a campaign to get each of our churches to raise a mile of pennies for the children's home.
>
> A year and a half later, six churches have reached their goal—a mile of pennies with a total of $5,068.80 for the home. In addition, 23 other churches are working toward their mile of pennies.
>
> Church members, friends, coworkers and neighbors are adding to the total as they take their daily walks, clean out their purses, pockets, dresser drawers and desks, looking for those almighty pieces of copper. People have donated shoe boxes, cans, jars, piggy banks and other types of containers filled with pennies that they have been saving for years. This has proved to be a terrific way to raise money.

Those people learned the value and importance of pennies,

but God already values you as an individual. And adding to our individual importance, we can band together with other Christians to make an impact in our world for Christ, just like a mile of pennies.

––––––––––

Precious Savior, thank You for being willing to shed Your blood even if I had been the only person alive. Help me to value myself as much as You value me. Amen.

40 / God Views You as Forgiven

Being forgiven means we are pardoned from the penalty of what we did wrong. The judge in charge of our case no longer desires to punish us or to hold our wrongdoing against us.

"In Him we have redemption through His blood, the forgiveness of our trespasses, according to the riches of His grace" (Eph. 1:7).

In January of 1982, 17-year-old Kevin Tunell killed 18-year-old Susan Herzog. He was later convicted in juvenile court of manslaughter and drunk driving. Susan's parents filed a suit for $1.5 million, which was settled for $936, of which Kevin must pay $1.00 every Friday until the year 2000.

For a little over a year, Kevin sent the $1.00 check faithfully to Susan's parents; but after that, he could no longer handle sending the money. It wasn't the money at all, but the constant reminder of the deed he had done.

As Christians, you and I are forgiven. Even though we should be sending our $1.00 every week to pay for our sins, God has designed a plan so that the amount has already been completely paid.

The problem comes when our enemy, Satan, tries to get us to continue sending our dollar payment as a lasting memorial to our shortcomings. As a result, we don't forgive ourselves, even though God has already forgiven us. Unlike Susan's parents, He doesn't want us to be continually reminded of our guilt.

Incredible God, You already have forgiven me. I praise You! Help me to forgive myself and stop beating myself up, because You aren't the source of those feelings. Amen.

41 / God Views You as Regenerated

Regeneration is when God gives us a new nature after we receive Jesus Christ into our life. It is what the Bible calls being "born again."

"He saved us, not on the basis of deeds which we have done in righteousness, but according to His mercy, by the washing of regeneration and renewing by the Holy Spirit" (Titus 3:5).

After Larry and I had been dating about 10 months, we decided we would visit each other's churches as a way of getting to know the other better. The first Sunday Larry attended my church. The following Sunday I went to his.

As I sat next to Larry in his church, I was intrigued. The people there seemed to be more loving than the people at my church, and they talked about God as if they knew Him personally. They also talked about being "born again" as the only method to become a true Christian. I had never heard of such a concept. After all, I knew I was a Christian. Didn't I go to church every Sunday, and hadn't I been born in a Christian nation? I figured that's what made a person a Christian. The pastor and laymen didn't say anything about that, but they did seem to have something I wanted: an intimate familiarity with God.

That morning, I left Larry's church with one thought: I wonder if I really am a Christian after all? That thought consumed my mind all that week.

The following Saturday evening, I went with Larry to see a Billy Graham film called *For Pete's Sake*, which told the story about a man who'd been "born again." After the movie ended, I wanted to go forward to find out more, but I was embarrassed. What would Larry think of me?

The next morning I returned to Larry's church with him and again admired the people's close relationship with God. I sat there thinking, I wonder whether I really am a Christian.

At the close of the service, the pastor asked the people to bow their heads and close their eyes. Then he asked, "Is there anyone here who's wondering whether they're a Christian?" I couldn't believe it! He had said the very same words I'd been thinking all week. How did he know?

Larry must have told him. Wait—I haven't even told Larry what I've been thinking.

In that moment, I knew God was trying to get my attention; and without thinking about it, I quickly raised my hand to indicate to the pastor I was the person he was talking about.

Then I realized what I was doing. Oh, no, I don't do weird things like this! I quickly took down my hand.

But the pastor had already noticed my hand; and after he dismissed the congregation, he came up to me with Wes Anderson, the new youth pastor at the church. They introduced themselves, and Wes took me and Larry back into his office.

Wes asked me a few questions, and I tried to explain that I wasn't sure I was a Christian. Wes replied, "Kathy, in order to become a Christian, you need to confess your sinfulness before God and ask Jesus Christ to forgive you and come into your life."

I said, "I want to do that, but I don't know how."

"If you'd like, I can say a simple prayer, and you can repeat it after me."

"Yes, please do."

Here's a prayer similar to the one I repeated on that special day of October 1, 1967: "Heavenly Father, thank You for loving me so much that You sent Your Son Jesus to die on the Cross for my sins. I open my heart's door and ask You to come into my life. Thank You for forgiving me and for making me Your child. In Jesus' name. Amen."

When I looked up with tears in my eyes, Wes asked me, "Where is Jesus now?"

I knew the right answer was that He was in my heart, but I couldn't believe it. It seemed too incredible that God would want to come into my unworthy life. But I didn't want to say the "wrong" thing, so I gave the right answer.

I left Larry's church that day still wondering if anything had happened to me. After all, no thunder had sounded from the sky, and no firecrackers had gone off in my mind. But as time went on and I learned more about living the Christian life, I could see that I was different. I had new desires and an assurance in my heart that Jesus was there. I had been regenerated, born again. In other words, my old sin nature had been replaced by God's righteous nature because the Holy Spirit had come to dwell inside me.

Has this happened to you? Have you opened your heart's door to ask Jesus in? You may have been reading this book and haven't understood all this business about being a Christian. Or maybe you sense something lacking in your life.

I have good news for you! Even though you've done wrong things that separate you from God, He still loves you. In fact, He loves you so much that He sent His Son, Jesus Christ, to die on the Cross at Calvary in your place. All you have to do is agree that you deserve to die spiritually but instead want to accept the gift of eternal life because of Jesus' death and resurrection.

Every person who becomes a Christian experiences his own unique way of making that commitment to God, but if you'd like to do it right now, you can. If the words of that prayer I said over 20 years ago are similar to your desires, you can say such words right now, and God will hear you. Please make that choice if you've never done so before. You don't even have to raise your hand!

————

Almighty God, thank You for the power of Your Spirit in washing clean the hearts of sinners and making their souls righteous in Your sight. You desire for every human being to make such a deci-

sion. May every person reading this book make sure she's made that decision. Amen.

42 / God Views You as Adopted

Being adopted is more than just being placed into a family. It is what enables a new family member to be considered a full adult heir.

"In order that He might redeem those who were under the Law, that we might receive the adoption as sons. And because you are sons, God has sent forth the Spirit of His Son into our hearts, crying, 'Abba! Father!' Therefore you are no longer a slave, but a son; and if a son, then an heir through God" (Gal. 4:5-7).

Although regeneration and adoption happen simultaneously in a new believer's heart, they give him separate qualifications. Regeneration brings him into the family; adoption qualifies him as heir to an inheritance.

Richard DeHaan says, "Every believer in Jesus Christ has also received the 'Spirit of adoption,' having been placed in God's family as an heir of all the riches in Christ. This is one of the great distinctions between the dispensations of law and grace. Under the law the people of Israel were treated like children, whereas under grace we are mature sons and heirs."[1]

Imagine that you're an orphan in a children's home, desperately wanting to be adopted. People come and go, but no one seems interested in you. Your heart is crushed. Your dreams are filled with images of being part of a wonderful, loving family who accepts you as you are.

One miraculous day a family arrives, and they point to you. "We want that special child." You look behind you, knowing they must be pointing to someone else. But there's no one behind you. "They're pointing to me! They want me!"

You cry with gratitude as the papers are signed and notarized. You climb into the car with your new family. They talk to you and smile at you. Your heart is bursting with joy. It's finally happened. You belong!

When you arrive at your new home, you're astonished at how large it is. They give you a tour of the rooms, and you're amazed at the immensity and the abundance of every convenience. Finally, they show you your room. Incredible. "A room to myself?" you ask. They confirm it's true.

That night as you lay in bed surrounded by warmth, both physically and emotionally, you can't believe your good fortune. But suddenly, you feel a sense of horror creep into your soul. "I don't deserve all this. I shouldn't be lying here so comfortably. I'm just adopted. Only the 'real' children should be taking advantage of all this."

With a sense of sadness, you climb down out of bed, make your way out of your room, out of the house, and out into the yard. Wandering around, you find the doghouse and crawl in to lie beside the family pet. Shivering from the cold, you finally fall asleep, tears dropping onto the dirt floor.

The next morning voices awaken you. The mother's voice shouts from a window. "Have you found her yet? She's not in the house."

From out in the yard, the father's voice replies, "No, I can't find her out here either. Keep looking. I hope she hasn't gotten lost."

You rub your eyes as the dog wags his tail and scoots out of the doghouse. You follow him and almost bump into the father's legs. Looking up, you see his startled look.

"What in the world are you doing here? Did you sleep in there?"

Before you can answer, he sweeps you up into the air, wraps his strong, warm arms around you, and carries you into the house. "Oh, you must be so cold. Let's get you bundled up."

Coming into the kitchen, you see the mother's face stare in surprise. "Where did you find her?"

Once everyone has sat down in the living room, you sit on the father's lap, staring at their concerned faces. The father gently asks, "Now, what is this all about? Why didn't you sleep in your room?"

At first you don't know how to form the words. But after a slight pause you say, "I can't sleep in that room."

"Why not?" the father gently asks. "Is there something wrong with it? Is there something else you need?"

"Oh, no. It's because I don't deserve anything so nice."

"Why do you think that? You know you've become a part of our family. Everything here is yours as well as ours."

"No, it's not. I'm just adopted. I don't deserve the same as your real children. It's just enough to know that you've adopted me. I don't need to have anything else."

A smile spreads over the father's and mother's faces. "Oh, we understand now. You think your adoption just got you into our family. You can't believe that you can now appropriate everything for yourself."

Your questioning look makes him stop. "What's appro-pr——?"

The father grins. "That's a big word to say 'to use' or 'call your own.' In other words, you didn't think you became our daughter, only our child. Honey, the truth is, not only did you join our family, but also you became entitled to everything that the rest of our sons and daughters enjoy. You are our real daughter."

With tears streaming down your cheeks, you jump out of the father's lap and twirl around in the center of the room. "All this is mine too. I'm your daughter. I can live like one of you!"

You run back to your father and throw your arms around his neck. "Thank you for adopting me! Thank you for giving me everything your other children enjoy!"

———

My Heavenly Father, thank You for entitling me to everything a true daughter or son deserves, even though I'm adopted. I'm so grateful, and I want to appropriate all of my spiritual and earthly blessings. Amen.

43 / God Views You with a New Name

A name is the word whereby each of us is identified and called. With it, someone can get our attention. A particular name, even though held by someone else, becomes special to us, as if it refers only to us.

"He who overcomes, I will make him a pillar in the temple of My God, and he will not go out from it anymore; and I will write upon him the name of My God, and the name of the city of My God, the new Jerusalem, which comes down out of heaven from My God, and My new name" (Rev. 3:12).

What's in a name? Ask the clerk at the Los Angeles Superior Court, where, for $108 plus the cost of a legal advertisement, anyone over the age of 18 can have his name changed.

Georgia Ricotta wanted her name changed. After all, who would want to be identified with a cheese? Her new name? Anna Novelli. "I picked my last name from a TV series," the new Anna says.

Clifford Morong also filled out the form and commented, "I dislike Morong, as it is often misspelled Moron." He came up with the name Cliff Michaels after looking through the telephone white pages.

Iranian-born Esmaeli Sabaghi Khiyabani said his birth name was too long and difficult. He wants to be called Oliver Twist.

"Nice, short names" are what Wittaya and Chuchai Mongkonsiriwatanas wanted. They became Witt and Gibb McDee.

The clerk who processes all the applications has already decided what her favorite new name request is: some man wanted to be renamed Zenith Ray Blitz. She comments, "I think he was in show business."

In these modern times, especially in the United States, usually a name is chosen because the parents like how it sounds. Few of us pick names for our children based on their meaning, and most of us don't even know what our name represents.

But that hasn't always been true.

The Israelites took naming persons . . . much more

seriously than we do today. To them a name was not just a label provided for convenience in distinguishing one person from another. A name was an essential part of the person so named. Names should be appropriate, for the person's name was regarded as a sort of duplicate or counterpart of its bearer; there was a mystical relationship between name and thing named. The name was conceived as influencing its bearer, and the name revealed something to a person who was told it. This was not a unique approach to naming, but one that prevailed among many ancient Near Eastern peoples.[1]

This fact seems to indicate Jesus' reasons for giving different names to some of the people involved in His kingdom. Simon became Peter, and Saul became Paul.

As God looks at you and me, He views us with the new name He has given us. Because we are "in Christ," we have a new identity.

Have you been a grumpy kind of person? Let God's grace make you "cheerful." Have you been a deceiver? Try God's new name, Israel: "one who strives with God" and prevails. Has your tendency been to be full of anger? God offers you the name, Love.

When we get to heaven, we will appreciate fully the beauties of our new identity. There we will rejoice that He molded us to His image as we "see him as he is."

———

Father God, I praise You for the new name You have granted me in Christ. May Your likeness radiate through it and may others be attracted to You. Amen.

44 / God Views You as Holy

To be holy means to be without sin. This lofty goal cannot be reached by humans on their own, only through the substitutionary death of Jesus Christ.

"Yet He has now reconciled you in His fleshly body through death, in order to present you before Him holy and blameless and beyond reproach" (Col. 1:22).

As a little girl, I always tried to be good. There was nothing I enjoyed more than to hear, "Oh, that Kathy, look at her. Isn't she sitting nicely? What a good little girl." I loved to be prim and proper and, of course, get some approval for it.

Several times as a preteen, my mother and I went to a retreat house for a weekend where nuns cared for all of us while we went to services, walked the beautiful grounds, or studied in the vast library. I loved staying there. I thoroughly enjoyed having my own little, sparse room to myself, since at home I had to share a bedroom with my sister. I soaked up the peaceful atmosphere and was able to leave all my worldly cares behind to concentrate solely on God.

The nuns seemed so peaceful and pure. It fascinated me to think of wearing the simple gold ring I saw on the nun's finger: to be married to God seemed like the most holy, unselfish, sanctified thing I could ever do. I observed the nuns through my youthful eyes and believed I saw saints. If anyone could be a saint, surely these women were it.

By the time I left, I'd made a commitment. I was going to become a nun! It seemed to me to be the only way to wipe away sin from my life. If I could just grow up, become a nun, and live in some retreat house, I'd be dedicated to God and safe from the evil and temptation that constantly made me feel guilty and unworthy of God's love.

As I grew up, some of my fascination with living the life of a nun dissipated as I realized that anywhere someone goes—even into a convent—there is sin and temptation. But inside I still longed for purity before God and to be wholly dedicated to Him in thought, word, and action.

When I fell in love with Larry as a senior in high school, I knew becoming a nun was out of the question! That ended that.

When I became a Christian at the age of 18, I didn't realize it immediately, but I had attained a relationship with God that set me on the journey of discipleship and holiness. With Christ's presence and grace in my life, without becoming perfect in judgment and without escaping to a sin-free environment, I had achieved the holiness I had sought as a child.

An illustration of this concept of holiness is found by examining a South American spider. This spider lives under the water by forming a bubble of air about itself and, like a diving bell, sinking to the bottom of a pond or river. Remaining there for hours, it breathes the air from above within the bubble. When it returns to the surface, it is perfectly dry, untouched by the water that surrounds it.

That's a picture of you and me. We are surrounded by the world and its sin and temptation. Yet, Christ has us in His bubble of holiness, and we are untouched by impurities in God's eyes.

Holy Father, I adore You for Your merciful desire to make me holy as You are holy. Knowing I'm holy in Your eyes makes me want to make wiser choices here on earth. Help me do that. Amen.

45 / God Views You as Righteous

To be righteous is to be considered without error or wrongdoing.

"And put on the new self, which in the likeness of God has been created in righteousness and holiness of the truth" (Eph. 4:24).

H. A. Ironside tells this story:

Years ago I was preaching in the small town of Roosevelt, Washington, on the north bank of the Columbia River. I was the guest of friends who were sheep-raisers. It was lambing time and every morning we went out to see the lambs—hundreds of them—playing about on the green. One morning I was startled to see an old ewe go loping across the road, followed by the strangest looking lamb I had ever beheld. It apparently had six legs, and the last two were hanging helplessly as though paralyzed, and the skin seemed to be partially torn from its body in a way that made me feel the poor little creature must be suffering terribly. But when one of the herders caught the lamb and brought it over to me, the mystery was explained. That lamb did not really belong originally to that ewe. She had a lamb which was bitten by a rattlesnake and died. This lamb that I saw was an orphan and needed a mother's care. But at first the bereft ewe refused to have anything to do with it. She sniffed at it when it was brought to her, then pushed it away, saying as plainly as a sheep could say it, "That is not our family odor!" So the herders skinned the lamb that had died and very carefully drew the fleece over the living lamb. This left the hind leg coverings dragging loose. Thus covered, the lamb was brought again to the ewe. She smelled it once more and this time seemed thoroughly satisfied and adopted it as her own.[1]

We were once like that orphaned lamb. We wanted to be accepted into God's family as His child, but we didn't have "the family odor." God wanted to adopt us but couldn't because we smelled of our own efforts and self-righteousness.

When we realized our striving to be good could never meet God's standard, we came to Him, humbly admitting our need as the angels in heaven rejoiced. God sacrificed the Lamb of God so that we could be covered by His robe, His "skin," of righteousness.

Now Jesus' robe makes us fit right in and even smell right! In fact, this aroma resembles the incense that encircles God's throne, praising Him for making it possible for us to join the flock with His righteousness.

———

Righteous Lord, I can only come before Your presence because Jesus' beautiful robe of righteousness covers every part of my life. Thank You for receiving me as Your own because of what Jesus did. Amen.

46 / God Views You as Blameless

Even though we've done many things wrong, God's acceptance of us as His children includes not being held accountable for the sins we've done.

"Just as He chose us in Him before the foundation of the world, that we should be holy and blameless before Him" (Eph. 1:4).

Are you like me? Do you blame yourself for everything? Over the years, I've developed an expertise about holding myself responsible for anything and everything. Did we plan a picnic and it rained? I must have done something to cause the weather to turn ugly. Did my child have a temper tantrum on the floor of the grocery store? Obviously, I must have pinched her. Did Larry arrive home from work grumpy? I must have displeased him in some way. My children not do their homework? I must be a terrible mother.

Going through life constantly blaming myself was a heavy burden to carry around. It reminds me of something I heard that happens in a foreign country named Abyssinia. When a man is convicted of an offense, he must be chained to a willing friend until he can pay the fine. Until then, the two connected men roam around, sharing one another's misfortunes, and if necessary, begging for the money to pay the fine so that they can regain their liberty.

What a vivid illustration of blame! It's like a constant burden that's chained to us, making joyful walking and living difficult. It flavors a person's view of life and creates resentment and insecurity.

It has taken me several years, even as a Christian, to realize that, from God's perspective, this "friend" called "blame" is no longer chained to my life. Now before I'm misunderstood, let me assure you that we do need to take responsibility for our sins. As Christians, 1 John 1:9 tells us to confess our sins and be cleansed from them. We should acknowledge when we do things wrong. What we're not supposed to do is continue to hit ourselves over the head for sins after we've been cleansed from them.

In one of my presentations I stress the need for us to stop saying, "I should have done that better," and instead say, "God, I ask You to forgive me. Next time, I'll do it differently." Or, "I'll learn from this mistake and trust God to empower me for the next time something like this comes up."

Changing our thinking from "I should have . . ." to "Next time I will . . ." relieves us of unnecessary negative self-talk that prevents us from appreciating the freedom from blame God has given us.

This process reminds me of a small article I read in the *Los Angeles Times* several years ago. It seems Paul and Susan Reid of Hartford, Conn., were out of their minds because they allowed their eight-year-old son, Ethan, to invite a few neighborhood friends over to color the walls of their house. Soon the walls of the two-story, four-bedroom house were covered with pink, blue, yellow, and purple chalk pictures, scribbles, and scrawls. The kids had a fantastic time, even taking pictures of their work as Paul and Susan enjoyed the children's artistic endeavors.

How could this be, you wonder? Well, you see, Paul and Susan had already arranged for painters to come in the next week and paint all the walls of their home.

Dear friend, you may be blaming yourself for the chalk on the walls, but God already knows the markings of your sin are painted over with the blood of Jesus. Obviously, I'm not going to carry the analogy to the extreme by saying God enjoys watching you sin. He doesn't approve of your sin, nor does He want you to sin, but He knows that you will have strong temptation in that direction. Yes, you should acknowledge when you've sinned, asking Him to forgive you. Accept His forgiveness and forgive yourself. You are blameless. He doesn't hold it against you.

Heavenly Father, thinking of Your view of me as blameless relieves my soul of the burden and bondage of not forgiving myself. I promise to not hold long accounts, since You don't either. Amen.

47 / God Views You as Predestined for Good Works

God plans, prepares, and puts into action the good works He wants us to do as His children.

"For we are His workmanship, created in Christ Jesus for good works, which God prepared beforehand, that we should walk in them" (Eph. 2:10).

My friend Michelle Cresse, author of several books, had flown into Canada to appear on a television show and to speak at several churches. As she stood in line for customs, she began to search through her purse, looking for her birth certificate and driver's license. "I know it's here," she muttered to herself. "I put it in here. Didn't I?"

She searched over and over again, but they were nowhere to be found. Panic flooded over her. "Did I pack it in my suitcase? What will happen now?"

By this time, it was her turn at the desk, and with a panicked look on her face she told the customs agent, "You're not going to believe this, but I can't find my identification. I thought I put my driver's license and birth certificate in my purse, but I can't find it. I'm afraid I must have packed it by mistake."

The man sighed. "Don't you have anything else? Anything with your picture and address on it will do."

Michelle thought hard. Picture . . . address . . . I can't think of any . . . Wait! I don't know if this will work or not, but I'll try.

Michelle reached into her briefcase and pulled out a copy of her book *Jigsaw Puzzles*, which deals with blended families learning to cope and adjust. "Sir, this is a book I've authored. It has my picture on the back, and in the printed biographical information, it says I live in the state of Washington. Will this do?"

The man looked at her and then at her picture. "Yeah, that's you, all right. Yes, I guess this will work. By the way, what's your book about?"

Michelle gave him a quick summary. He replied, "I've been

married for seven years, and now I can't stand my wife. I've stayed with her because of my five-year-old daughter. What do you think I should do?"

Michelle gulped. Glancing at the line of hundreds waiting to pass through customs, she sent up a quick prayer and jumped into answering his question, suggesting that he should look at the underlying causes of his dissatisfaction and try to work on them. She gently pointed out to him that statistics showed that even if he divorced his wife, he'd most likely remarry someone with the same problems.

That caught his attention, and he asked her more questions. By the time they'd finished their conversation, Michelle had given him a copy of her book and he'd promised to read it, even though she'd explained it was written from a Christian perspective.

As Michelle walked away, she praised God for such an unusual and divine opportunity and thought, *Lord, I'm not qualified to share in my own power, but with You and me together, I am qualified and empowered.*

Michelle could have had no idea her trip would include such a chance meeting. But God knew all along and indeed had planned such an encounter for His praise and glory. He knows beforehand the works that you and I will do as His special children. We are His workmanship, created for special works, many of which are surprises and blessings.

You may be wondering what happened to Michelle's identification. The next time she looked into her purse, she found her driver's license and birth certificate immediately.

———

Creative God, I praise You for the privilege of fulfilling the plans You have in mind for me. Thank You for using me, even though I'm unworthy of being used. To You belongs the praise and glory. Amen.

48 / God Views You as Protected

God is in control of our lives; therefore, nothing can happen to us except what He allows and means for good. He defends us and guards us from evil, even though we have an enemy, Satan.

"My prayer is not that you take them out of the world but that you protect them from the evil one" (John 17:15, NIV).

Charlie Wedemeyer, a former high school and college football star and Hawaii's Athlete of the Decade for the 1960s, cannot breathe on his own, can't move any of his muscles himself, can't hold up his head, and can't speak. Now in his middle 40s, Charlie was diagnosed with Lou Gehrig's disease (amyotrophic lateral sclerosis) over 13 years ago and was given about 3 years to live. He's still alive and praising God.

He's not just existing, he's living! Charles fulfills many speaking engagements by having his wife, Lucy, read his lips and speak for him. Charles is good at making audiences laugh, and he doesn't even say a word. Everyone who meets him comments that his eyes almost speak for him, through a wink, a stern gaze, a wide-open look of amazement. Lucy says, "The perfect way to keep Charlie quiet would be to shave off his eyebrows."

What does Charlie say about his life? Lucy's voice interprets, "I can see now how much God has used me, and in so many different ways. We have been able to visit and share with so many various groups—other ALS patients, first graders to senior citizens, all sorts of people. It is nice that He has enabled me to have some impact on all these people. I love my life."

His son, Kale, a former high school football star, says of his dad, "I can't keep my dad in the house." Indeed, one of the problems of the Wedemeyer household is finding enough for Charlie to do. He loves to go shopping—especially for clothes—and out to dinner. He has frequent speaking engagements, traveling all over the country. He has attended every one of Kale's track meets and football games.

Charlie wants to pack life to the fullest. "After all," he reasons, "people with a terminal disease tend to be depressed and give up; but if you think about it, it's all terminal because there are no promises for tomorrow for anyone.

"So many people dread the thought of getting up when the alarm rings at six o'clock in the morning, but they should be glad to get out of bed. We tend to take those things for granted and not appreciate what we have. I thank God every day that I can see and hear and be able to breathe through this machine and get nourishment through these tubes."

Charlie Wedemeyer is a living, breathing example of God's protection. It may not appear that he's the best example of how God views us as being protected because usually our thinking concludes if we're protected, nothing bad will happen to us.

But listen to Jesus' words: "These things I have spoken to you, that in Me you may have peace. In the world you have tribulation, but take courage; I have overcome the world" (John 16:33).

Jesus said we would have tribulation in this world. The apostle Peter wrote, "Beloved, do not be surprised at the fiery ordeal among you, which comes upon you for your testing, as though some strange thing were happening to you; but to the degree that you share the sufferings of Christ, keep on rejoicing; so that also at the revelation of His glory, you may rejoice with exultation" (1 Pet. 4:12-13).

Someone once reminded me that Jesus prayed for His disciples to be delivered from evil; He didn't pray for them to be delivered from testings. I wonder whether evil can be defined as when testings overwhelm us and make us stop trusting God. Evil is when Satan wins. That only happens if we stop being empowered by the Holy Spirit in our response to temptations, testings, afflictions, and trials.

These problems of life actually are used by God for good. David wrote, "It is good for me that I was afflicted, that I may learn Thy statutes" (Ps. 119:71).

David recognized the value of having unfortunate circumstances in his life. He didn't say God wasn't protecting him. On the contrary, he constantly called God his Shield and Fortress.

But if we have the attitude that God's protection means we won't be tested, we can easily begin to believe God doesn't view us as protected.

One of the visual aids I often use during my speaking engagements is a cheesecloth. Modern brides don't often use a cheesecloth other than for cleaning and dusting. But a cheesecloth used to be valued by cooks in times past as a filter to strain foods. As I hold up my cheesecloth while speaking, I talk about how it can represent God's filter of love that protects us from anything He doesn't want us to experience. First Cor. 10:13 says, "No temptation has overtaken you but such as is common to man; and God is faithful, *who will not allow you* to be tempted beyond what you are able, but with the temptation will provide the way of escape also" (italics mine).

God's cheesecloth filter of love wrapped around our lives doesn't allow any circumstance or experience except what He intends for our good and what we can resist in His power.

Just ask Charlie Wedemeyer. He's convinced God's protection surrounds him and that He has used his difficulties for good.

――――――――

Faithful Lord, I thank You for the protective guard of Your love, which filters out and prevents anything from entering my life that is not in Your plan for me. You don't create bad circumstances, but sometimes You do allow them in my life for the development of my dependence on You. I'll trust and thank You even then. Amen.

49 / God Views You as Unified with Him and Other Christians

Being at one with each other as Christians means we have the same purpose and goals, striving for His glory and the spread of the gospel throughout the world.

"I do not ask in behalf of these alone, but for those also

who believe in Me through their word; that they may all be one; even as Thou, Father, art in Me, and I in Thee, that they also may be in Us; that the world may believe that Thou didst send me. And the glory which Thou hast given Me I have given to them; that they may be one, just as We are one" (John 17:20-22).

Most of us have been in situations where disagreement has surfaced within a Christian organization or group. Disagreements and differences of opinion are not bad or wrong in themselves, but at times they become ammunition for Satan to create division and disunity. Jesus wants us to be unified.

How can we aspire to greater unity within the brethren? Let's write a scenario in our imaginations.

The deacon board is gathering tonight for the monthly meeting of the First Evangelical Church in Somewhere, U.S.A. Immediately, tension fills the meeting room. There's a controversial issue they must discuss and decide.

The chairman calls the meeting to order and leads in a short word of prayer, asking the Lord to be with them to guide them. Each member gives his opinion, and within minutes the debate is intensifying. There are two camps, and they are bitterly opposed to each other, each believing the other is wrong.

Suddenly, in the midst of this confusion and raised voices, the door opens, and the Lord Jesus walks in. "Thank you for asking Me to come. Now, where would you like Me to sit?"

Someone offers a chair, and Jesus sits down, the room filling with silence. "Well, go on with whatever you were doing."

Everyone stares sheepishly at the table, but the chairman clears his throat and opens up the discussion again. Now the voices are subdued and courteous, yet the tension remains.

Jesus' voice breaks in. "You each really want to convince the other of your position, don't you?"

"Why, of course, Lord," one man interjects. "That's what we're here for. We must stand for certain principles."

"Yes, of course, that's correct. My Word does have principles that must be followed."

Another man speaks up. "Lord Jesus, as I'm sure You're

aware, this particular issue doesn't have a specific principle in Your Word; that's why we're so at odds."

Jesus smiles and nods. "Yes, that's difficult. Therefore, I'd like you to try something different. Would you?"

Each man looks across the table with a perplexed expression. In their hearts, most of the men do not want to try anything different; they enjoy the debate and challenge of convincing others of their opinion. Several enjoy expounding their ideas eloquently, thus feeling superior when another tries lamely to express his ideas. One man finds it satisfying to appear humble because of his slow, soft speaking; yet everyone knows once his acid tongue finishes, they will all feel knocked down to size. One man loves to quote Scripture verses that he feels verify his position, yet he really just wants to show how many verses he has memorized.

But how could they object to Jesus' suggestion? They hesitantly nod.

Jesus' calm voice starts, "Please close your eyes and bow your heads. You really want to do the best, yet you feel confident your position is the right one. I'd like you to try to empty yourself as much as possible of your own opinion."

Most of the men shift in their seats uncomfortably. Two raise their heads to protest, but when Jesus meets their gaze with a smile, they smile back and again close their eyes.

Then in the silence of the room, Jesus begins to speak to each man's heart individually. To each it sounds like the room is vibrating with His voice, yet they know He's speaking within their minds.

"Joe, I love you, but you are basing your position on your own insecurities because of your childhood abuse."

"Tom, you are My servant, yet you are thinking in terms of wanting everyone's approval, rather than looking to Me."

"Carl, you are trying to find unconditional acceptance from others without first getting it from Me. I accept you totally."

"Rick, you are very zealous for My cause, but a spirit of humility, even when there is strong disagreement, is the spirit on which I smile."

Jesus' words pierced their souls, one by one. More than a few wiped their eyes.

Gradually, each one's heart surrendered to God's will and emptied itself of its own agendas, willing to do whatever Jesus wanted. In the subdued and tolerant discussion that followed, someone suggested a compromise that had not been discussed or considered before. Immediately, they knew they'd found the solution. Each one would be required to give away a portion of his position, but the solution would be acceptable and godly. Why hadn't they thought of it before? they wondered.

This scenario borders on the perfect, granted, but I'd like to think we could learn to be more tolerant toward others if our own insecurities and blocks to hearing God were wiped away.

First Pet. 4:8 tells us, "Above all, keep fervent in your love for one another, because love covers a multitude of sins."

If we love our fellow believers, unity will result—a kind of unity that is patient with others' mistakes; a compassion for another's weaknesses because we're all a part of the Body. Within that love, there is a lack of desire for revenge or bitterness. Within unity there is room for discipline.

If we can surrender our own ideas and be willing to do whatever Jesus wants, we'll grow closer to that goal of unity.

The next meeting of Christians you go to, why not suggest a chair be left empty, symbolizing Jesus' presence. It'll be a good reminder.

———

Unified Trinity, empower me to lay aside my own insecurities that I might hear Your voice and leading. Help me to remember how much You want Your Body to be unified and healthy. Amen.

50 / God Views You as a Steward

As Christians, our possessions are not really ours. They actually belong to God, and He has allowed us to manage them with His direction.

"Is it not lawful for me to do what I wish with what is my own?" (Matt. 20:15).

I wasn't handling the situation very well at all. Larry and I had bought a product for a little over $1,000 from a Christian business, and when they could not deliver the product, they promised us a refund in 10 days. The 10 days came and went, but Larry and I left on vacation, so we set the matter aside. When we returned home, the refund still had not arrived. We called the business and left a message after they told us the owner was out of the country. Two weeks passed, no return call. We called again. He was in a meeting. We left another message.

The following week, an employee of the company returned our call and wanted to know all the details. He would let his boss know and get back to us. Nothing happened. We began to wonder what was going on. Would we ever get our money? It had been almost two months since the refund had been promised. How in the world could a Christian man be giving us the runaround? Christian people didn't act like this. The company was located in Florida; we lived in California. What could we do?

The situation began to possess my mind. The thought of it barged into my thoughts during the day and woke me up at night. The unfairness of it infuriated me. It wasn't just the money. It was the principle of the thing! *God, how can You allow this? Convict this man of his sin!*

One day during my devotions, my thoughts again turned to the situation. Anger welled up inside of me. I wrote in my journal:

> This is a trial and a test of whether we really trust the Lord and believe in His righteousness and justice. How we respond about this will show whether we've truly surrendered our possessions to God. We say we're just stewards; are we going to be owners now?
>
> That doesn't mean we shouldn't try to do something about it. We should. But more important is our attitude. If we become angry and anxious, that is an indication that we regard the money as our own. If we trust God for the outcome and emotionally release the money, that's an indication we regard it as God's loss.
>
> God *is* righteous and just. He can replace the money

in another way if He wants us to have it. If not, He is in charge of the judgment of others. My anger—which wells up in me as we place fruitless and impotent phone calls—can be replaced by trust in the Lord. Praise the Lord.

I took several deep breaths and sensed the Lord wanting me to release again this whole situation to Him. I continued writing. "Father God, this is not hidden from Your sight, and neither are Your eyes closed and uncaring. Thank You, Lord, that I can surrender all my cares to You."

It occurred to me that it might be helpful for me to memorize some verse that pertained to my struggle. In my inner being, I sensed the Lord say, "Turn to Jer. 17:5-8." I answered, *Lord, You know I've been memorizing those verses, and they have nothing to do with this situation. You must be mistaken.*

I began to flip through the New Testament, thinking I'd surely find some passage or verse referring to these circumstances. But nothing looked interesting or pertinent. *Oh, all right, Lord. I'll look at Jer. 17:5-8, but it won't do any good.*

I turned to the Jeremiah passage; but before I could find the exact verses, my eyes locked on to a verse right at the top of the page that I'd marked in yellow who knows when. It was Jer. 16:17, and it said, "For My eyes are on all their ways; they are not hidden from My face, nor is their iniquity concealed from My eyes."

I couldn't believe it. That was almost the same words I had written down in my prayer! Tears filled my eyes, and it seemed to me God had spoken directly to me. He did care. He was noticing what was happening. I could trust Him.

Peace flooded my heart. I am the steward, not the owner, and the Owner is aware of the situation. I won't be held in bondage by anger and resentment. God is in control.

I memorized Jer. 16:17. Every time the situation began to make me angry, I repeated that verse and reminded myself that God was aware, and He cared.

Over the following month, Larry and I made calm decisions using righteous means to try and get the money returned. We were willing to never have the money if that was God's will, but we also felt Him leading us to make some efforts even as we kept a right attitude. After further stalling by the company, the money was finally refunded. We were very relieved and appreciated having the money.

As we reflected on this incident, we realized afresh that we are the stewards for the money God has given us, not the owners.

———

Righteous Heavenly Father, You are aware of everything that happens in my life, and You care. Thank You that You promise to provide for all my needs, according to Your riches in glory in Christ Jesus. Amen.

51 / God Views You as His Ambassador

An ambassador represents the country or king of the country from which he comes. An ambassador, when viewed by others, would seem to be similar to the king he represents.

"Therefore, we are ambassadors for Christ, as though God were entreating through us; we beg you on behalf of Christ, be reconciled to God" (2 Cor. 5:20).

> Dr. J. Wilbur Chapman, a famous evangelist from the past, said that the New Testament records tell of 40 people, each suffering from the same disease, who were healed by Jesus. Of this number, 34 were either brought to Jesus by friends, or He was taken to them. In only six cases out of 40 did the sufferers find the way to Jesus without assistance. Of the vast number of people who find their way to Jesus today, most of them reach Him because the friends of Jesus are concerned about the welfare of their souls.[1]

Although many people come to know the Lord just by reading the Bible, most are brought to Him through another Christian. I don't know why God chooses to use you and me as His beacons, lighting the way to salvation, but that's exactly what He's done. It is an awesome responsibility that He's entrusted to us.

As ambassadors for Christ, we represent what God is like and who He is. Sometimes we don't do a very good job of that. Our reflection of Jesus is muddied. It reminds me of a man who walked through a large art gallery with some friends, wanting to display his knowledge of pictures. Unfortunately, he had forgotten his glasses, but that didn't stop him. Standing before a large frame, he began, "This frame is altogether out of keeping with the subject and as for the subject itself, it is altogether too homely, in fact, too ugly, ever to make a good picture. It is a great mistake for any artist to choose so homely a subject for a picture if he expects it to be a masterpiece."

The gentleman went on and on until his wife finally could fit in a word. "My dear, you are looking into a mirror."[2]

When I watch the television news, at times an ambassador from another country will be interviewed. As I hear him talk and express his views, I make the assumption that his statements represent the ruler of his country and the attitudes of his people.

When unbelievers hear what you and I say as Christians—as ambassadors of Christ's kingdom—they assume we represent Jesus' views. I can look back over my 24 years of knowing Christ and cringe at some of the statements I've made, thinking I spoke God's truth. Now I realize I wasn't quite accurate or completely informed.

Even with the possibility of our not being perfect ambassadors, we should not hesitate to speak out and take whatever action God is directing. Yes, we'll make mistakes because we're human, but we can still represent Christ in the best way we can, thus becoming that "sweet aroma of the knowledge of Him in every place" (2 Cor. 2:14).

A child hearing the verse "We are made a spectacle . . . to angels, and to men" (1 Cor. 4:9, KJV) prayed, "O Lord, please keep Your spectacles clean so that sinners can see You through us, 'cause You know, Lord, we are Your spectacles."[3]

Although we know that word doesn't refer to eyeglasses, that child's interpretation does remind us that if our lives are godly and represent our King Jesus, we, His ambassadors, will help "foreigners" see a picture of Him that's not blurred.

Almighty God, it's an amazing thought to comprehend that You've chosen me to be Your ambassador, representing You and speaking on Your behalf. May I get to know You so well that I can give an accurate representation of You. Amen.

52 / God Views You as Seated in the Heavenly Places

As Christians, we have the power to see life from an eternal perspective, because our real "place" is in heaven.

"And raised us up with Him, and seated us with Him in the heavenly places, in Christ Jesus" (Eph. 2:6).

As a former zookeeper at the Los Angeles Zoo, Gary Richmond tells the story of how he once came across a small cage filled with 15 beautiful red-tailed hawks. They had been caught illegally by some criminals and had been held for a long time at the zoo in case they were needed for evidence at the court trials. Gary's ire was raised at the horrible way these birds were forced to live and decided he must take things into his own hands. He decided to free them by opening the cage door when no one was around, confident he would only receive a small reprimand for the "accident." He relates what happened:

> After one hour I decided to check the cage. Astonishment, disbelief, wonder, and confusion reigned supreme as I beheld all 15 birds still in the cage relaxing. There was still time. Perhaps the red-tails just needed some inspiration. Well, I knew what would be inspirational. I ran into their cage waving my arms and growled like a bear. That inspired them, all right. They flew out of the cage and

landed not 10 feet from the cage door. The look that they gave me was pitiful. They were confused and it was clear to me that they wanted back into the cage. "Don't you see the sky?" I pleaded. "That's what you were meant for." I began feeling a little self-conscious inside the cage so I stepped out to finish my address. "What's wrong with you? You're not chickens. You're majestic birds of prey. You hunt your food. God gave you a purpose, now go fulfill it." I decided to go back to the health center. Maybe their instincts would take over and they would feel some primal urge to command the wind. I left for 15 minutes and then returned. Not one bird had felt any urges. In fact, some had walked back into the cage. With 15 minutes to go, I gave up. I don't mind telling you I was more than a little deflated. I ended up herding the birds back into the cage like goats. Where had I gone wrong?[1]

Sometimes I wonder whether God could ask that same question in relation to us, His children. He's made us qualified to sit with Him in the heavenly places and to be citizens of heaven, yet we more often choose to live like citizens of the world, just like those majestic red-tails preferred to live like chickens. We're created in Christ Jesus to soar through the skies of great faith and bold works, but instead we mutter and grumble, wondering whether we have enough power for God to work in our lives.

Sometimes I feel like Moses was talking about me when he analyzed the Israelites' behavior by saying:

> Yet you were not willing to go up, but rebelled against the command of the Lord your God; and you grumbled in your tents and said, "Because the Lord hates us, He has brought us out of the land of Egypt to deliver us into the hand of the Amorites to destroy us. Where can we go up? Our brethren have made our hearts melt, saying, 'The people are bigger and taller than we; the cities are large and fortified to heaven. And besides, we saw the sons of the Anakim there'" (Deut. 1:26-28).

I grumble in my tent when I think things like, God doesn't love me, or else He wouldn't be allowing such trying experiences in my life. If He really meant good for me, He would make my life perfect so that I wouldn't have to struggle.

Other times, I stoke the fire in my tent and lament, I don't have enough faith to do what God wants me to do. The non-Christians He wants me to share my faith with don't want to hear what I have to say. Their minds aren't opened. They'll debate me down. They're too powerful and intelligent for me.

Yet, God has given me the opportunity of sitting with Him in the heavenlies, thereby being empowered by Him to do whatever He wants me to do. What's the solution? It's in Deut. 1:30-31: "The Lord your God who goes before you will Himself fight on your behalf; just as He did for you in Egypt before your eyes, and in the wilderness where you saw how the Lord your God carried you, just as a man carries his son, in all the way which you have walked, until you came to this place."

The solution is to remember that God has good intentions for us and plans on protecting, empowering, and carrying us through our wilderness into the Promised Land.

During those times when I grumble in my tent, I can remind myself God doesn't expect me to be perfect, just excellent: living up to the realistic expectations He has for me and the work He wants me to do.

———

Heavenly Father, thank You that You're willing to teach me to live with You in the heavenlies. In Your eyes, I'm already there, but right now I'm learning to do that more often. Amen.

53 / God Views You as Sealed with the Holy Spirit

God, through grace, has put His seal upon us. He has also given the Holy Spirit to us as a pledge toward our future stay in heaven.

"In Him, you also, after listening to the message of truth, the gospel of your salvation—having also believed, you were sealed in Him with the Holy Spirit of promise, who is given as a pledge of our inheritance, with a view to the redemption of God's own possession, to the praise of His glory" (Eph. 1:13-14).

Tom Rees says,

> In Canada I have watched the lumberjacks felling the mighty trees. The first thing they do is seal the timber— brand it with their peculiar mark as their private property. After this it is floated downriver, and on the lakes it is gathered in booms ready for the sawmill. Each log is immediately identified by its seal. God chose you for himself and purchased you through the blood of his Son; on the very day you committed your life to Jesus Christ, God sealed you by giving you the gift of his Holy Spirit. Every child of God bears the same seal, is indwelt by the same Holy Spirit.[1]

Not only is the seal of the Holy Spirit a symbol of ownership like the one branded onto wood, but it can also be illustrated by the seal used to notarize a document or to secure an envelope or a scroll (as in the apostle Paul's time).

Unger's Bible Dictionary instructs us that a seal was
> a portable instrument used to stamp a document or other article. . . . The impression made therewith had the same legal validity as an actual signature, as is still the case in the east. Indeed, the importance attached to this method is so great that, without a seal, no document is considered authentic. In a similar manner coffers, doors of houses and tombs, were sealed.[2]

When I was a teenager, I enjoyed going to the stationery store and buying sealing wax and a fancy metal monogram tool. After writing my letter, I would carefully melt the wax onto the flap of the envelope and then quickly push the metal monogram into the soft wax, making a delicate design. The letter seemed even more important and special with that touch of extra effort and beauty.

In times past, letters didn't have gum-sealed envelopes, so wax was used as a way of indicating whether the enclosure had been opened prematurely. A friend of mine closes his letters, not with "Sincerely Yours," but with the words "Without Wax," and then signs his name. I think it's his way of saying that what he has written is genuine, open, and available to be viewed by any and all.

Paul's careful use of the word "sealed" in Ephesians 1 gives us several insights into its application for our lives. By the seal of the Holy Spirit, we, as Christians, can know we are:

- secure—God does not break His covenant.
- authentic—the design inlaid in the wax indicates that only one monogram tool was used by the person owning it.
- approved—a seal was used only after the owner verified the information within the letter or on the document as acceptable to him.
- genuine—a monogram tool's design was unique and one of a kind, owned by one individual.
- identified as belonging to God—such a seal indicated the owner who had sent the document or letter.

In times past, often the tool used to put the design into the wax was actually the head of a ring that the king or person in authority constantly wore. No wonder his particular seal was authentic and genuine. He didn't let it out of his sight. If he gave someone permission to use the ring, they had the same power he did.

Our modern-day notary stamp is like the old-time seal. It authenticates and makes the document valid, thus holding accountable the people signing the document.

Additionally, Eph. 1:13 and 14 tell us the Holy Spirit is a "pledge" given to us by God. Another word for pledge is "deposit" (NIV). The Holy Spirit is a deposit toward what we will fully receive in heaven. Of course, we receive the fullness of the Holy Spirit, but our experience with Him on this earth is only a taste, a sample, of the glory we will receive as we stand in the presence of God.

This kind of deposit or pledge is a bestowal of His grace and is a guarantee of more to come. "In essence, the 'deposit' of the Holy Spirit is a little bit of heaven in believers' lives with a guarantee of much more yet to come."[3]

Generous Lord, thank You for the gift of Your Holy Spirit. I'm looking forward to spending eternity with You in heaven, knowing the deposit of Your Spirit is only the beginning of the glory we'll share. Amen.

54 / God Views You as Precious

Although all of God's creations are important to Him, the most significant and precious thing is mankind. God was willing to use something more precious than gold or silver—the blood of His Son, Jesus—to redeem mankind.

"Knowing that you were not redeemed with perishable things like silver or gold from your futile way of life inherited from your forefathers, but with precious blood, as of a lamb unblemished and spotless, the blood of Christ" (1 Pet. 1:18-19).

Imagine for a moment that you are on the streets of Jerusalem at the time of Jesus' triumphal entry as the Messiah. The crowd is buzzing with excitement. Thousands are choked into the small avenues of the city and the outlying areas. Rumors have been flying through the crowd all morning. "Jesus is on His way to declare His Messiahship."

Finally in the distance, you hear a mounting roar. Jesus is coming. A feeling of electricity spreads through the crowd. As the noise grows closer, someone shouts, "There He is. There's Jesus, riding a donkey's colt."

Standing on your tiptoes, you finally see Him. He's sitting regally upon the donkey, smiling at the praises toward Him as the Messiah. You hear your own voice shouting out, "Hosanna! Hosanna! Praise to the Messiah!" You're waving the palm branch that someone has handed you, but you're so far back in the crowd, you despair of having the privilege of setting it down so that Jesus can be transported over it.

Oh, if only, I could get closer. I want Him to know I'm praising Him. I want Him to know I believe He's my Messiah.

He's coming closer now, and the noise is incredible. Everyone is trying to get His attention. "Hosanna! Hosanna!"

How can He hear my voice with everyone else calling out? If only I could get closer. If I could just have Him look at me and know I'm here. Then I'd be sure He knows I truly want to believe.

Wait. Maybe I don't want Him to see me. I'm so sinful. I'm just a nobody. How can I even think that He'd notice me with so many important people surrounding Him?

By now Jesus' donkey is in front of the crowd before you, and He's scanning the crowd with a calm, confident smile. You can tell He's absorbing the praise, and it seems absolutely appropriate. Your arms are swinging back and forth, the palm branch making a half circle above your head, as you hope He'll look over and give you a passing glance.

What's this? Jesus has stopped His donkey. Yes, it's true. He's getting off, and it looks like He's walking toward you. Me? Can't be. There's so many people around. He must be looking for someone else. He can't even know I'm here. I've never met Him before. But look, He is coming in my direction, right toward me, and everyone is making a path for Him, even as they keep right on praising Him. Incredible!

With a broad smile on His face, He walks up to you and reaches out His hands to lay them gently on your shoulders. A deep peace settles in your soul. If you'd known something like this was going to happen, you would have anticipated being terrified, but there is no fear in you. Your soul is melted into love and surrender as Jesus' eyes look deeply into yours.

He seems to know everything about me, but I feel His unconditional love and acceptance. He knows me! He knows everything about me, yet He still loves me!

Then His golden voice speaks, and even though the crowd is tumultuous in their praise, His words are clear in your ears. "My child, I love you. I forgive you for all your wrongdoings, and I want to give you the power to live obediently to Me. I'm going to die soon, but just remember that I'm dying for you so that you can be reconciled to God. If you were the only person alive, I would still be dying just for you. You are precious in My sight."

You stand in awe and soak up each word. His attention seems completely normal and expected. You don't understand everything He's said, but there's an inner knowledge that everything will be revealed eventually.

You whisper, "Thank You," but Jesus is instantly back on the colt, continuing His way through the crowd. A cocoon of love surrounds you as you calmly wave good-bye. You will never be the same. *I am loved. He knows who I am, and I'm precious to Him. That's all I need.*

————

All-knowing God, I praise You for Your ability to make me feel special and distinct from so many other people. I am important and precious to You. Thank You for knowing and yet accepting me. Amen.

55 / God Views You as Rich

The riches God gives me may not be completely evident here on this earth, but they are being stored for me in heaven.

"I pray that the eyes of your heart may be enlightened, so that you may know what is the hope of His calling, what are the riches of the glory of His inheritance in the saints" (Eph. 1:18).

Now that we've come to the end of this book and have learned about the awesome inheritance we have in Christ, I hope you feel rich! For indeed, we are rich beyond compare with so many fabulous privileges as a child of God. The riches we have named are only the beginning. Hopefully, this will whet your appetite to want to learn more about these privileges—and responsibilities—we have since joining God's family.

I can see that our examination of these joys could result in several reactions. First, we might feel let down. If I'm so rich in this inheritance, then why can't I be perfect now? Why can't I live life abundantly as Jesus promises in John 10:10? Why is life still a struggle?

I can understand your frustration, for I've experienced it myself. All we can do is understand that God has not finished writing the book of our life yet. God is still at work on it, and it won't be finished until we reach heaven. We were never meant to experience the fullest degree of these blessings on this earth. There's a future attainment that will be ours completely in heaven.

We might also ask ourselves, "If I know I'm so rich in God's spiritual provisions, why is money still such a temptation to me? Why can't I be satisfied with what I have?"

For most of us, that's a question that can only be solved by God waving a magic wand over us, removing the desire for earthly wealth. Yet, He chooses not to do that, so we struggle, even though we're already wealthy spiritually.

We know Benjamin Franklin was right when he said, "Money never made a man happy yet, nor will it. There is nothing in its nature to produce happiness. The more a man has, the more he wants. Instead of it filling a vacuum, it makes one. 'Better is little with the fear of the Lord, than great treasure, and trouble therewith.'"[1] We know money won't make us happy, but we'd sure like to find out for ourselves by getting some!

Ray O. Jones gives an interesting evaluation of money's hold on us by telling us what a dollar says to us:

> You hold me in your hand and call me yours. Yet may I not as well call you mine. See how easily I rule you? To gain me, you would all but die. I am invaluable as rain, essential as water. Without me, men and institutions would die. Yet I do not hold the power of life for them; I am futile without the stamp of your desire. I go nowhere unless you send me. I keep strange company. For me, men mock, love and scorn character. Yet, I am appointed to the service of saints, to give education to the growing mind and food to the starving bodies of the poor. My pow-

er is terrific. Handle me carefully and wisely, lest you become my servant, rather than I yours.[2]

Another consideration: God may not wave that magic wand over us because our material riches or lack of them serve a purpose. Charles Caldwell Ryrie, in his book *Balancing the Christian Life,* gives this perspective: "How we use our money demonstrates the reality of our love for God. In some ways it proves our love more conclusively than depth of knowledge, length of prayers or prominence of service. These things can be feigned, but the use of our possessions shows us up for what we actually are."[3]

So money does have a purpose in our lives. Through it, God tests our priorities and gives us a nibble at the wealth we'll experience in heaven. Just think of how it feels to have some extra cash in your hand and the bills are all paid. Now magnify that feeling a million-fold: that's how we'll feel when we can fully appreciate the spiritual riches of heaven.

Hopefully, we experience a little of that even as we meditate on the abundant riches we have in Christ as a part of our inheritance. Complete fulfillment will come in heaven, but with the taste we have now, it certainly makes heaven even more desirable.

In the last devotion about our view of God, titled "God Is God," I mentioned Exod. 33:13, where Moses prayed for the ability to know God. In verse 17, God answered Moses. What He says to Moses is God's word to you and me because of our position in Christ: "And the Lord said to Moses, I will do this thing also that you have asked, for you have found favor, loving-kindness and mercy in My sight, and I know you personally and by name" (Amp.).

Beloved child of God, what riches we have! God knows us personally and by name.

———

Wealthy God, thank You for Your generosity in sharing Your wealth of the inheritance we have in Christ. We look forward to its complete fulfillment in our heavenly mansion. Amen.

Notes

INTRODUCTION

1. J. I. Packer, *Knowing God* (Downers Grove, Ill.: InterVarsity Press, 1973), 30.

DEVOTION 1

1. Sherwood Eliot Wirt and Kersten Beckstrom, *Topical Encyclopedia of Living Quotations* (Minneapolis: Bethany House Publishers, 1982), 148.

DEVOTION 2

1. Paul Lee Tan, *Encyclopedia of 7,700 Illustrations* (Rockville, Md.: Assurance Publishers, 1979), 679.

DEVOTION 4

1. *Moody Monthly* (Jan. 1988), 14-15.
2. George Sweeting, *Great Quotes and Illustrations* (Waco, Tex.: Word Books, 1985), 95.

DEVOTION 6

1. Dick Eastman, *A Celebration of Praise* (Grand Rapids: Baker Book House, 1984), 143.
2. Ibid., 144.

DEVOTION 8

1. A. W. Tozer, *The Knowledge of the Holy: The Attributes of God: Their Meaning in the Christian Life* (New York: Harper and Brothers, Publishers, 1961), 73.
2. Merrill F. Unger, *Unger's Bible Dictionary* (Chicago: Moody Press, 1957), 80.

DEVOTION 10

1. Tozer, *Knowledge of the Holy*, 115.
2. Ibid., 117-18.

DEVOTION 12

1. Ibid., 45-46.

DEVOTION 14

1. Packer, *Knowing God*, 73-74.
2. Ibid., 75.

DEVOTION 16

    1. Ibid., 80.

    2. Tozer, *Knowledge of the Holy*, 66.

    3. Ibid., 68.

DEVOTION 17

    1. David C. Needham, *Close to His Majesty* (Portland, Oreg.: Multnomah Press, 1987), 56.

    2. Emery H. Bancroft, *Elemental Theology* (Grand Rapids: Zondervan Publishing House, 1955), 53.

DEVOTION 18

    1. Needham, *Close to His Majesty*, 63.

    2. Ibid., 64-65.

DEVOTION 19

    1. Ibid., 36.

DEVOTION 20

    1. Tozer, *Knowledge of the Holy*, 89-90.

    2. Wirt and Beckstrom, *Living Quotations*, 79.

    3. H. A. Ironside, *Illustrations of Bible Truth* (Chicago: Moody Press, 1945), 34-35.

DEVOTION 21

    1. Herbert Lockyer, *All the Doctrines of the Bible* (Grand Rapids: Zondervan Publishing House, 1964), 31.

    2. Tozer, *Knowledge of the Holy*, 112-13.

    3. Ibid., 114.

DEVOTION 22

    1. Eastman, *Celebration of Praise*, 127.

    2. Ibid.

    3. Tan, *7,700 Illustrations*, 493.

DEVOTION 23

    1. Gary Richmond, *A View from the Zoo* (Waco, Tex.: Word Books, 1987), 16-17.

    2. Packer, *Knowing God*, 129-30.

    3. Eastman, *Celebration of Praise*, 94.

DEVOTION 24

    1. Bancroft, *Elemental Theology*, 43.

    2. Ibid., 44.

    3. Tozer, *Knowledge of the Holy*, 59.

DEVOTION 25

    1. Richmond, *View from the Zoo,* 174-75.

DEVOTION 27

    1. Packer, *Knowing God,* 136.
    2. Needham, *Close to His Majesty,* 132-33.
    3. Packer, *Knowing God,* 139.

DEVOTION 28

    1. Ibid., 153.
    2. Ibid., 155.
    3. Ibid., 155-56.

DEVOTION 29

    1. Eastman, *Celebration of Praise,* 31.
    2. Tozer, *Knowledge of the Holy,* 41, 43.

DEVOTION 33

    1. Packer, *Knowing God,* 96.

DEVOTION 35

    1. John Bisagno, *God Is* (Wheaton, Ill.: Victor Books, 1983), 71.

DEVOTION 37

    1. Tan, *7,700 Illustrations,* 1226.

DEVOTION 38

    1. Ibid., 1187.

DEVOTION 41

    1. Unger, *Unger's Bible Dictionary,* 843.
    2. *Vine's Expository Dictionary of Old and New Testament Words,* 138.

DEVOTION 44

    1. Richard DeHaan, *The Living God* (Grand Rapids: Zondervan Publishing House, 1967), 186.

DEVOTION 45

    1. Madeleine S. Miller and J. Lane Miller, *Harper's Encyclopedia of Bible Life* (San Francisco: Harper and Row Publishers, 1978), 92.

DEVOTION 46

    1. John F. Walvoord and Roy B. Zuck, eds., *The Bible Knowledge Commentary* (Wheaton, Ill.: Victor Books, 1983), 333.

Devotion 48

    1. Ironside, *Illustrations of Bible Truth,* 33.

Devotion 54

    1. Tan, *7,700 Illustrations,* 1614.
    2. Ironside, *Illustrations of Bible Truth,* 92.
    3. Ibid., 32.

Devotion 55

    1. Richmond, *View from the Zoo,* 49.

Devotion 56

    1. Wirt and Beckstrom, *Living Quotations,* 111.
    2. Unger, *Unger's Bible Dictionary,* 989.
    3. Walvoord and Zuck, *Bible Knowledge Commentary,* 619.

Devotion 58

    1. Tan, *7,700 Illustrations,* 830.
    2. Ibid., 823.
    3. Charles Caldwell Ryrie, *Balancing the Christian Life* (Chicago: Moody Press, 1969), 84.